The Cambridge Guide to VisiCalc

BOB MOULD & FRAN TEO

The Cambridge Guide to VisiCalc

Cambridge University Press

Cambridge

London New York New Rochelle

Melbourne Sydney

Published by the Press Syndicate of the University of Cambridge
The Pitt Building, Trumpington Street, Cambridge CB2 1RP
32 East 57th Street, New York, NY 10022, USA
10 Stamford Road, Oakleigh, Melbourne 3166, Australia

First published 1985

Printed in Great Britain at the University Press, Cambridge

Library of Congress catalogue card number: 84-14976

British Library Cataloguing in Publication Data

Mould, Bob
The Cambridge guide to VisiCalc

1. VisiCalc (Computer program)
I. Title II. Teo, Fran
001.64'25 HF5548.4.V57

ISBN 0 521 31902 1

TG

CONTENTS

APPENDIXES

ACKNOWLEDGEMENTS

The authors wish to thank the following friends and colleagues for their help:

Andrew Hills for “test-driving” the tutorial section, pointing out a number of inconsistencies and outright mistakes in the text, and for helping simplify the occasional over-complicated explanation.

Duncan Lowery for providing the templates for most of the chapter on technical templates and for producing the biorhythms template in the Fun with VisiCalc chapter.

1

What's a "spreadsheet"?

"Spreadsheet" is the modern name for the time-honoured accountant's analysis sheet, where paper and pencil (and eraser!) were employed to help analyse sales into categories, to calculate the payroll, to analyse overdue invoices, and so on. Originally, all the calculations were done by hand. Clerical labour was cheap and no-one was in any great hurry for the results of the analyses. The invention of the mechanical desk calculator (remember them? – they whirred and rattled and made a great fuss but they could be faster than mental arithmetic in many cases) – helped to get the answers right first time by eliminating most of the sources of calculation error. However, recalculation of an analysis sheet, just because a few figures had changed, was still a tedious time consuming exercise. Even the advent of the electronic calculator hasn't removed this tedium or made any really significant improvement in calculation speed. Only the arrival of cheap computing power has made any real difference to the speed of analysis. Now a complete recalculation of a complex analysis sheet can be made literally in seconds, making "I wonder what the result would be if..." questions much easier to answer.

Imagine a very large sheet of paper divided into 63 columns and 254 rows (making 16 002 boxes or 'cells'). This is the 'spreadsheet' or analysis sheet. Such a sheet of paper would typically be around four feet wide and four feet deep – rather large and unwieldy! Imagine also that it is pinned up on the wall with a TV camera pointing at it. This camera is capable of displaying only part of the sheet – about four or perhaps eight columns wide and twenty rows deep – on a TV screen on the other side of the room. Imagine also that the TV camera is remotely controlled. Now substitute your computer's memory for the sheet of paper and your computer display screen for the TV (of course you may be using a TV as a computer display). The computer keyboard takes the place of pencil and eraser and there you have the electronic spreadsheet. No modern businessman should be without one!

The uses of a spreadsheet are limited only by the

imagination of the user, but the actual size of the sheet is limited by the memory available in your computer in which to hold the information 'written' onto the sheet. Unless you are fortunate enough to be using the very latest in desktop microcomputers you are very unlikely to be able to cope with a large sheet without splitting it into several smaller ones. However, this is not the problem it sounds. With a little forward planning it is possible to cope with any size of sheet by splitting it into several smaller ones and by linking these smaller sheets together using data files.

The real power of a spreadsheet, however, lies in the computer's ability to recalculate the complete sheet each time one or more figures are changed. And, what's more, it can do it in only a few seconds. A really large complex sheet may take as much as 30 seconds and this is regarded as being rather a long time! So you can see that the "what if..." type questions can be answered almost instantly. By hand such answers could take perhaps half a day or longer to obtain, and how many businessmen can afford to be tied up for so long? Shortage of the time necessary to do the planning essential to a successful business results in "guesstimates" being made which, at worst, may be wildly incorrect and at best not as good as they might have been.

So in what areas of a business can spreadsheets be used? The answer is "almost everywhere". Financial applications are perhaps the most obvious. Applications such as cash flow planning, gross margin analysis (including allowance for currency variations where raw materials or finished goods are imported, or sales are priced in a foreign currency), stock taking valuation and so on are common. However, it is also possible to plan the load on a factory week by week and to explore the effects on capacity of a potential order. Product design calculations can be performed using spreadsheets, provided the calculations do not involve higher mathematics such as differential calculus and stick to such things as trigonometrical functions and logarithms. Teachers would find a spreadsheet useful when called upon to produce analyses of class test and exam results. Perhaps a rather neglected area is that of business studies. Quite realistic business games can be run using exactly the same spreadsheets as the businessman uses. As was said before, the only real limitation is that of imagination. If it can be done on a paper analysis sheet then it can be done on its electronic equivalent, only much, much more quickly.

2

Introduction

This book is divided into two main sections. The first part shows you how to construct a working spreadsheet (the worksheet) and introduces many of VisiCalc's facilities as and when they are required. Because VisiCalc can be used on a variety of computers it is assumed you are acquainted with your own computer, and with details such as how to load VisiCalc into your computer, which keys move the VisiCalc cursor, which key deletes the last character typed, how to name a worksheet when it is to be saved on floppy disk and so on. It would be impossible to explain all the computers on which VisiCalc can be used but the Apple II, Apple IIe and CP/M based computers are covered in appendix A. However, it's recommended you have the VisiCalc manual appropriate to the computer you are using readily available. It's also strongly recommended you follow through the training example by building up your own version. The old training adage

> "What I hear, I forget.
> What I see, I remember.
> What I do, I understand."

most definitely applies here!

The second part of this book deals with templates. A template is a worksheet all set out with column headings, fixed data, formulae, etc., ready to receive current data such as this month's sales and so on. A number of tried and tested templates are included here.

The training section sets out to build up a simple payroll worksheet from scratch. It uses successive additions to the same example as it progresses and the final result looks something like this:

TAX RATE % 30

JOB GROUP	TAX CODE	EMP. NUMB.	EMP. NAME	HOURLY RATE	HOURS WORKED	GROSS PAY	FREE PAY	TAX DUE	NET PAY	OLD YEAR-T-D GROSS PAY	OLD YEAR-T-D TAX PAID	NEW YEAR-T-DATE GROSS PAY	NEW YEAR-T-DATE TAX PAID
1	193	0052	BROWN	1.50	37.20	55.80	37.12	5.61	50.19	55.80	5.61	111.60	11.21
2	240	0098	GREEN	1.60	40.00	64.00	46.15	5.35	58.65	64.00	5.35	128.00	10.71
3	432	0133	BLACK	1.95	36.50	71.18	83.08	0.00	71.18	71.18	0.00	142.35	0.00
4	278	1432	WHITE	2.01	42.20	84.82	53.46	9.41	75.41	84.82	9.41	169.64	18.82
3	345	1545	JONES	1.95	37.30	72.74	66.35	1.92	70.82	72.74	1.92	145.47	3.80
3	654	2386	VANCE	1.95	28.00	54.60	125.77	0.00	54.60	54.60	0.00	109.20	0.00
2	231	2912	EVANS	1.60	38.50	61.60	44.42	5.15	56.45	61.60	5.15	123.20	10.31
1	510	3005	KING	1.50	39.40	59.10	98.08	0.00	59.10	59.10	0.00	118.20	0.00
1	488	3112	BAKER	1.50	38.25	57.38	93.85	0.00	57.38	57.38	0.00	114.75	0.00
2	325	3610	SMITH	1.60	29.70	47.52	62.50	0.00	47.52	47.52	0.00	95.04	0.00
			TOTALS		367.05	628.73	710.77	27.44	601.29	628.73	27.44	1257.45	54.87
			AVERAGE		36.71	62.87	71.08	2.74	60.13	62.87	2.74	125.75	5.49
			MAXIMUM		42.20	84.82	125.77	9.41	75.41	84.82	9.41	169.64	18.82
			MINIMUM		28.00	47.52	37.12	0.00	47.52	47.52	0.00	05.04	0.00

JOB GP	RATE/HR.
1	1.50
2	1.60
3	1.95
4	2.01
5	2.43

3

Getting started – labels and values

Load VisiCalc so that it displays an empty VisiCalc worksheet on the screen. The top left corner displays the co-ordinates of the cell at which the cursor currently is placed, and also displays the contents of that cell (at present the cell is totally empty so there are no contents to be displayed). The top right hand corner diplays the letter "C". This indicates that recalculation of the worksheet will take place column by column. Below this is a figure which indicates how much memory is available for your worksheet (measured in "K", where 1K represents 1024 bytes of memory or about 1024 characters) – the bigger the better since really useful worksheets can use a lot of memory. Command prompts will be displayed on line 2 and whatever you type on line 3. Line 3 is called the edit line. Line 4 contains the column names "A", "B", etc. right up to "BK", i.e. 63 columns. The left hand side of the screen displays the row numbers, from 1 to 254. Thus there are 63 × 254 cells available in VisiCalc. How many of them are usable in practice depends primarily on the amount of memory available in your computer and then on the complexity of any formulae and the lengths of the column headings and other textual matter.

Into each cell may be typed either a "label" or a "value". A label is a collection of characters such as a person's name or a column heading. Arithmetic cannot be performed on a label – indeed it would be ridiculous to try! As it happens, VisiCalc treats a label as if its arithmetic value were zero, so that if a label cell is accidentally (or sometimes on purpose) included in a calculation, then a value of zero is assumed for that cell and little or no harm is done. A value may be either a number, or a formula which calculates a number based on the values placed in other cells. VisiCalc recognises whether what is being typed into a cell is to be treated as a label or as a value or formula by examining the first character typed.If it is a letter, then a label is assumed. Anything else (except ") indicates a value. If a label starts with a non-alphabetic character, then VisiCalc must be told to treat the characters typed as a label by typing a quote symbol (") as the first character of the label. The quote symbol is not part of the label, it is merely an attribute of the cell containing the label. Similarly, if a formula starts with an alphabetic character a numeric symbol (such as +) must be placed in front of the formula to tell VisiCalc to treat the characters being typed in as a formula (i.e. the cell will have a "value" attribute). To move from cell to cell in the worksheet use the cursor controls (arrow keys) as specified in the VisiCalc manual appropriate to your particular computer. Usually it is self-evident which are these keys.

To illustrate labels, values and formulae try the simple example. If you make a complete mess of typing into a cell, merely press "return" (or whatever your computer uses instead) and start typing the cell contents afresh. The new data will overwrite the old data completely when either "return" or a cursor control is next pressed. Don't be afraid to experiment! You can't do any lasting harm to anything. The very worst that can happen is that you lose all the information you have so laboriously typed in, but this is rare, thank goodness.

```
Fig. 1       A        B         C          D          E
     1  EMP.     EMP.      HOURLY     HOURS      GROSS
     2  NUMB.    NAME      RATE       WORKED     PAY
     3  0052     BROWN            1.5        37.2
     4
     5
```

Rather untidy! The reason that the numbers don't line up with their column headings is that labels ("text") are left justified (i.e. start at the left of the cell, spare blanks being on the right) and numbers are right justified (spare blanks on the left). VisiCalc cannot "centre justify" either labels or numbers. Remedying this fault involves using formatting commands.

Formatting commands act both on an individual cell ("local"), or on the whole worksheet ("global"). Labels in the column headings may be right justified by placing the cursor on the cell containing the label and then typing /FR. As soon as the / is typed, a prompt line

```
''COMMAND: BCDEFGIMPRSTVW-''
```

will appear. Each of these letters represents a command

which may apply to a cell, to a complete row or column of the worksheet or to the worksheet as a whole. "F" means "Format". As soon as the "F" is typed, a second prompt line will appear

```
FORMAT: D G I L R $ *
```

The "L" means "left justify" and the "R" means "right justify". The others refer to formatting numbers and will be explained later. Typing "L" or "R" causes instantaneous justification of the cell contents. All the cells containing labels may be right (or left) justified in one fell swoop by typing the command /GFR. "G" means "global". Numbers may be formatted as integers (ie whole numbers) or in "pounds and pence" format (actually dollars and cents format). Any other number of decimal places must be programmed into a formula (see Hints and tips section of this book).

```
Fig. 2   A        B         C          D       E
    1     EMP.     EMP.    HOURLY    HOURS   GROSS
    2    NUMB.    NAME       RATE    WORKED    PAY
    3     0052    BROWN      1.50     37.20
    4     0098    GREEN       1.6        40
    5
```

To format the numbers in line 3 of fig. 2, place the cursor on each cell containing the number to be formatted and type /F. The prompt

```
FORMAT: D G I L R $ *
```

will be displayed. "G" means "general" and causes all the decimal places needed to display a number completely to be displayed on the screen, provided there is enough space in the cell. "I" means "integer" – the number will be displayed as a whole number with no decimal point or decimal places. "$" means "pounds and pence" or "dollars and cents" format – i.e. to two decimal places including any trailing zeroes that may be necessary. "*" is a special format used to display a bar-chart instead of numbers, and "D" ("default") removes any local cell formatting. Formatting then reverts to whatever global format commands are in force for the worksheet as a whole. Local formats override global ones. Having formatted the numbers in line 3, (using /F$) type in the information for line 4. The employee numbers in column A will only be displayed with leading zeroes if you type them in preceded by a quote (") to ensure VisiCalc treats them as labels, not as numbers.

Now format the numbers in line 4. You should now have a worksheet similar to the following:

```
Fig. 3   A        B         C          D       E
    1     EMP.     EMP.    HOURLY    HOURS   GROSS
    2    NUMB.    NAME       RATE    WORKED    PAY
    3     0052    BROWN      1.50     37.20
    4     0098    GREEN      1.60     40.00
    5
```

To calculate gross pay in column E, place the cursor at cell E3. A quick way to do this is to type 〉E3 and then press "return". "〉" means "go to" and "E3" are the cell co-ordinates. The value which should appear in the gross pay column for employee number 0052 is obtained by multiplying the hourly rate (in cell C3) by the hours worked (in cell D3). The formula for this is +C3*D3. "*" ("star" or "asterisk") means multiply – there's no conventional multiply symbol on a computer keyboard that wouldn't be confused with the letter "x". Similarly, divide is indicated by a / ("slash" or "oblique stroke") symbol. So, type +C3*D3 in cell E3. The gross pay will be calculated immediately, but it will not be pounds-and-pence formatted – yet. Format the result using /F$. Now do the same for line 4, only the formula will now be +C4*D4. The rest of the worksheet could be typed up in the same way, but it would be unnecessarily hard work. Luckily, it is possible to pre-format cells which will receive numeric data and to copy formats and formulae to anywhere on the worksheet. It is fortunately also possible to adjust copied formulae to allow for their new positions in the worksheet. These features of VisiCalc will be covered in the next chapter.

Meanwhile, it is a good idea to save your worksheet as it stands at present on floppy disk. This is done by typing /SS and supplying a file name (how about using "PAY3"?). /S is the storage command. Typing /S produces the prompt

```
STORAGE: L S D Q #
```

"L" means "load a worksheet from disk", "S" means "store a worksheet on disk", "D" means "delete the stored version from the disk", "Q" means "quit VisiCalc" (the current worksheet will be destroyed – so save it first if you want to come back to it), and "#" means "use the special Data Interchange Format (DIF) when storing on disk or loading from disk". Some computers also include "I" meaning "initialise" a brand new disk. "Initialising" a disk means preparing it for use. So /SSPAY3 will store the current worksheet on floppy disk under the name PAY3. The allowable names for files vary from computer to computer, so consult the VisiCalc manual for your computer to find out what naming retrictions apply in your case. If your computer uses the CP/M operating system, then you should preface the file name with "B:" if you wish to store the file on the "B" disk drive. If you are using an Apple with two disk drives, then ",D2" should be appended to the file name.

RECAP

A LABEL begins with a letter.

A FORMULA begins with a number or a mathematical symbol such as + - * / ( ) % $ etc.

" (quote) makes what would otherwise be a number or formula into a label.

* (star) is the multiply symbol.

/ (slash) is the divide symbol and starts a command.

/FR and /FL right and left justify text in individual cells.

/GFR and /GFL right and left justify all the cells on the whole sheet.

/FI formats individual values (numbers or the results of calculations) as integers (whole numbers).

/F$ formats values in pounds-and-pence (or dollars and cents) form.

/FG gives the number of decimal places needed to express the number accurately within its cell width.

/FD removes any local format and reverts to the global format. Local formats take precedence over global formats.

/SS stores a worksheet on floppy disk. For file naming conventions, see your particular VisiCalc manual. CP/M restricts file names to not more than eight characters, but the Apple can cope with much longer file names.

4

Formatting and replicating

If you quit VisiCalc at the end of chapter 3, load VisiCalc back into your computer and re-load the saved worksheet. To do the latter, type /SL followed by the name you stored it under. When loading is complete, you should see on the screen exactly what was on it when you saved the worksheet, even down to the position of the cursor. You are now ready to continue adding to the worksheet.

Before typing in any more hourly rates or hours worked it would be sensible to pre-format the cells so that these figures appear in pounds-and-pence format automatically. To do this for the rates column, place the cursor in cell C5 (Try using 〉C5). Now format this blank cell using /F$. This formatted blank cell must now be copied ("replicated" is the VisiCalc term) down the rest of the column (as far as row 14 in this example). This is done by placing the cursor on the cell to be copied (it should already be there) and then typing /R. The current cell co-ordinates will appear on the edit line (line 3 of the display) and the prompt

```
Replicate: Source range or RETURN
```

will appear on line 2. The source range can be a single cell, a row of cells or a column of cells. The range is specified by giving the co-ordinates of the first and last cells of the row or column, separated by a dot. VisiCalc turns this dot into an ellipsis (i.e. three dots...). Since only one cell is to be copied (replicated) just press return. The prompt

```
Replicate: Target range
```

will appear on line 2. Now type the co-ordinates of the first cell of the range into which you wish to replicate the source cell (C6), then type a dot (again this will be converted into an ellipsis), then type the co-ordinates of the last cell in the range (C14). Finally, press return. Nothing will appear to happen, but if you examine the contents of, say C10, (i.e. place the cursor at C10 by using ⟩C10 for example) you will see that the cell has been formatted using /F$. Numbers typed into any of these formatted cells will appear in pounds-and-pence style automatically. Now do the same for column D. After typing in the data for row 5, your worksheet should now look something like fig. 4.

Fig. 4	A	B	C	D	E
1	EMP.	EMP.	HOURLY	HOURS	GROSS
2	NUMB.	NAME	RATE	WORKED	PAY
3	0052	BROWN	1.50	37.20	55.80
4	0098	GREEN	1.60	40.00	64.00
5	0133	BLACK	1.95	36.50	71.18
6					
7					

To replicate the gross pay formula, place the cursor on cell E5. The formula +C5*D5 will appear on line 1. Now type /R as before. Since only one cell is to be replicated, press return. The target range is E6 to E14. A further prompt will appear asking you whether you wish to copy the co-ordinates C5 into E6, E7 etc. without adjustment (N for No change), or whether C5 should become C6 in line 6, C7 in line 7 and so on, (R for Relative). Here the formula should be adjusted to suit the row it is copied into (ie answer 'R'). The same question will be asked concerning cell D5. A column of zeroes should appear in column E row 6 and below. Now place the cursor on one of these cells and satisfy yourself that the formula has indeed been copied correctly. Your worksheet should now look something like fig. 5.

Fig. 5	A	B	C	D	E
1	EMP.	EMP.	HOURLY	HOURS	GROSS
2	NUMB.	NAME	RATE	WORKED	PAY
3	0052	BROWN	1.50	37.20	55.80
4	0098	GREEN	1.60	40.00	64.00
5	0133	BLACK	1.95	36.50	71.18
6					0.00
7					0.00
8					0.00
9					0.00
10					0.00
11					0.00
12					0.00
13					0.00
14					0.00
15					0.00

Now type in the missing data to produce a worksheet something like fig. 6. Note that employee numbers are treated as labels (remember to press " as the first character), that the hourly rates and hours worked are displayed automatically in pounds-and-pence format and that the gross pay is calculated immediately.

Fig. 6	A	B	C	D	E
1	EMP.	EMP.	HOURLY	HOURS	GROSS
2	NUMB.	NAME	RATE	WORKED	PAY
3	0052	BROWN	1.50	37.20	55.80
4	0098	GREEN	1.60	40.00	64.00
5	0133	BLACK	1.95	36.50	71.18
6	1432	WHITE	2.01	42.20	84.82
7	1545	JONES	1.95	37.30	72.74
8	2386	VANCE	1.95	28.00	54.60
9	2912	EVANS	1.60	38.50	61.60
10	3005	KING	1.50	39.40	59.10
11	3112	BAKER	1.50	38.25	57.38
12	3610	SMITH	1.60	29.70	47.52
13					0.00
14					0.00
15					

It would be a good idea to save this worksheet now (as PAY6 perhaps?) using /SS. Try changing a few figures to see the effect. Don't try to change directly any of the calculated figures such as gross pay – if you do, you'll destroy the formula in that cell.

RECAP

FORMAT a complete column (by using /F$ and /R) before entering data which is to appear in pounds-and-pence format.

ENTER a formula only once and use /R to copy ("replicate") that formula down the rest of the column. Cell co-ordinates in the formula may be retained "as is" ("No change") or may be altered automatically to relate to the row or column containing the destination cell ("Relative").

5

Totalling, more calculations and replication, inserting a row

Re-load the worksheet you saved at the end of the preceding chapter. If it's still on the screen and you've made any changes, you will need to clear the screen first by typing /C (followed by Y to acknowledge that you really meant to do so, and that /C was not just an accident). Then the saved version may be re-loaded.

VisiCalc provides a number of built-in funcions to perform such tasks as totalling, averaging, counting, etc. All begin with the symbol "@" and all are of the same basic form, so once you understand totalling, the other functions are obvious since they work in the same way. In the following example, place the cursor at B15 and type the label "TOTALS". To calculate the total hours worked, place the cursor at D15 and type @SUM(D3.D14). The dot will be replaced by an ellipsis (...) by VisiCalc. This will add the contents of cells D3, D4, D5,....to D14. It is the logical equivalent of +D3+D4+D5+D6+D7+D8+D9+D10 +D11+D12 +D13+D14, but occupies much less memory and is much quicker to type in. Format D15 using /F$. Now do the same for the gross pay column. The result should look something like fig. 7.

Fig. 7	A	B	C	D	E
1	EMP.	EMP.	HOURLY	HOURS	GROSS
2	NUMB.	NAME	RATE	WORKED	PAY
3	0052	BROWN	1.50	37.20	55.80
4	0098	GREEN	1.60	40.00	64.00
5	0133	BLACK	1.95	36.50	71.18
6	1432	WHITE	2.01	42.20	84.82
7	1545	JONES	1.95	37.30	72.74
8	2386	VANCE	1.95	28.00	54.60
9	2912	EVANS	1.60	38.50	61.60
10	3005	KING	1.50	39.40	59.10
11	3112	BAKER	1.50	38.25	57.38
12	3610	SMITH	1.60	29.70	47.52
13					0.00
14					0.00
15		TOTALS		367.05	628.73
16					
17					

Lines 13 and 14 are available, already formatted, to accept two more employees.

The next step is to calculate the tax due from each employee, and hence his or her net pay. Assume for the time being that everyone pays tax as a flat percentage of their gross pay. In order that "What if..." calculations can be made to assess the implications of a tax rate change, it will be a good idea to arrange for the current tax rate to occupy a cell of its own and for it not to be built into any formulae as a fixed value ("hard coded" is the jargon phrase). Perhaps the logical place to put the tax rate is at the head of the tax due column, but currently there is no space there. To make space, a blank row needs to be inserted above the current row 1. To do this, place the cursor anywhere on row 1 and type /I (I = Insert). The prompt "Insert: R C" will appear. Type R (for Row. C means insert a blank column at the cursor position). A blank row will appear as row 1 and what was row 1 will now be row 2 and so on. All the formulae involved will have been adjusted to allow for the insertion. Any global formats in force will apply to this new line as well, but no local formats have yet been specified. In cell E1 type "TAX RATE%", format cell F1 to display numbers as integers (/FI) and type in the tax rate of 30 (%). Don't try to type the % sign after the 30 – you'll get an error message. To left justify the actual tax rate so that it appears close after the % sign, add an extra local format of /FL. Now type in the column headings "tax due" and "net pay". The result should look something like fig. 8.

Fig.8	A	B	C	D	E	F	G
1					TAX RATE % 30		
2	EMP.	EMP.	HOURLY	HOURS	GROSS	TAX	NET
3	NUMB.	NAME	RATE	WORKED	PAY	DUE	PAY
4	0052	BROWN	1.50	37.20	55.80		
5	0098	GREEN	1.60	40.00	64.00		
6	0133	BLACK	1.95	36.50	71.18		
7	1432	WHITE	2.01	42.20	84.82		
8	1545	JONES	1.95	37.30	72.74		
9	2386	VANCE	1.95	28.00	54.60		
10	2912	EVANS	1.60	38.50	61.60		
11	3005	KING	1.50	39.40	59.10		
12	3112	BAKER	1.50	38.25	57.38		
13	3610	SMITH	1.60	29.70	47.52		
14					0.00		
15					0.00		
16		TOTALS		367.05	628.73		
17							
18							

The tax due for the first employee (Brown) should appear in cell F4 and is calculated by multiplying the gross pay by the tax rate, the formula being +F1*E4/100. The result must also be formatted using /F$. This formula is then replicated down the rest of column F using /R. The source range is just F4. The target range is F5 to F15. In this case, F1 is actually wanted, unchanged, in each cell but E4 must be adjusted to be E5 on row 5, E6 on row 6 and so on. So type "N" for "No change" when "F1" appears in inverse video and "R" for "Relative" when "E4" appears in inverse video. The result should look like fig. 9. If it doesn't, you've probably replicated the formula in cell F4 incorrectly.

Fig.9	A	B	C	D	E	F	G
1					TAX RATE % 30		
2	EMP.	EMP.	HOURLY	HOURS	GROSS	TAX	NET
3	NUMB.	NAME	RATE	WORKED	PAY	DUE	PAY
4	0052	BROWN	1.50	37.20	55.80	16.74	
5	0098	GREEN	1.60	40.00	64.00	19.20	
6	0133	BLACK	1.95	36.50	71.18	21.35	
7	1432	WHITE	2.01	42.20	84.82	25.45	
8	1545	JONES	1.95	37.30	72.74	21.82	
9	2386	VANCE	1.95	28.00	54.60	16.38	
10	2912	EVANS	1.60	38.50	61.60	18.48	
11	3005	KING	1.50	39.40	59.10	17.73	
12	3112	BAKER	1.50	38.25	57.38	17.21	
13	3610	SMITH	1.60	29.70	47.52	14.26	
14					0.00	0.00	
15					0.00	0.00	
16		TOTALS		367.05	628.73		
17							

Now add in the formula to calculate net pay, format the cell and replicate it down the net pay column. (The formula and commands needed appear after the next picture of the worksheet.) To total the tax due and net pay, either replicate the gross pay totalling function in cell E16 into F16 and G16, or type the appropriate @SUM function into each of E16 and F16. The worksheet should now look something like fig.10.

The net pay formula for the first employee is +E4-F4. The replication command is /R. The source range is just G4 alone and the target range is G5 to G15. Replication will, of course, be relative.

Now save this version of the worksheet for later use (/SS PAY10).

Fig.10	A	B	C	D	E	F	G
1					TAX RATE % 30		
2	EMP.	EMP.	HOURLY	HOURS	GROSS	TAX	NET
3	NUMB.	NAME	RATE	WORKED	PAY	DUE	PAY
4	0052	BROWN	1.50	37.20	55.80	16.74	39.06
5	0098	GREEN	1.60	40.00	64.00	19.20	44.80
6	0133	BLACK	1.95	36.50	71.18	21.35	49.82
7	1432	WHITE	2.01	42.20	84.82	25.45	59.38
8	1545	JONES	1.95	37.30	72.74	21.82	50.91
9	2386	VANCE	1.95	28.00	54.60	16.38	38.22
10	2912	EVANS	1.60	38.50	61.60	18.48	43.12
11	3005	KING	1.50	39.40	59.10	17.73	41.37
12	3112	BAKER	1.50	38.25	57.38	17.21	40.16
13	3610	SMITH	1.60	29.70	47.52	14.26	33.26
14					0.00	0.00	0.00
15					0.00	0.00	0.00
16		TOTALS		367.05	628.73	188.62	440.11
17							
18							

RECAP

/IR inserts a blank row at the cursor position and adjusts any formulae affected by pushing the cursor row and the rows below the cursor down one row. The formulae on and below the cursor row are adjusted as necessary.

/IC inserts a blank column at the cursor position, pushes the cursor column and all columns to the right of it one column further to the right and adjusts the formulae involved to reflect the new cell co-ordinates.

/R replicates a source range of cells into a target range of cells, adjusting each cell co-ordinate (if required) so that it is correct for the particular row or column into which it is being replicated. Replication is a form of copying. So far, the source range has been a single cell and the target has been a range of adjoining cells.

@SUM (start...end) totals the range of cells commencing with "start" and ending with "end". "Start" and "end" must either be in the same column or the same row.

/FI formats a cell to display a number as an integer.

/FL left justifies the displayed cell contents.

6

Tidying up the sheet

As it stands at present, the worksheet is not as neat looking as it could be. A few horizontal lines in the appropriate places would improve its appearance considerably as you can see from this example:

```
Fig.11     A        B        C        D        E        F        G
    1                                     TAX RATE % 30
    2-----------------------------------------------------------------
    3     EMP.     EMP.   HOURLY    HOURS    GROSS      TAX      NET
    4    NUMB.     NAME     RATE   WORKED      PAY      DUE      PAY
    5-----------------------------------------------------------------
    6     0052    BROWN     1.50    37.20    55.80    16.74    39.06
    7     0098    GREEN     1.60    40.00    64.00    19.20    44.80
    8     0133    BLACK     1.95    36.50    71.18    21.35    49.82
    9     1432    WHITE     2.01    42.20    84.82    25.45    59.38
   10     1545    JONES     1.95    37.30    72.74    21.82    50.91
   11     2386    VANCE     1.95    28.00    54.60    16.38    38.22
   12     2912    EVANS     1.60    38.50    61.60    18.48    43.12
   13     3005     KING     1.50    39.40    59.10    17.73    41.37
   14     3112    BAKER     1.50    38.25    57.38    17.21    40.16
   15     3610    SMITH     1.60    29.70    47.52    14.25    33.26
   16                                         0.00     0.00     0.00
   17                                         0.00     0.00     0.00
   18-----------------------------------------------------------------
   19            TOTALS            367.05   628.73   188.62   440.11
   20=================================================================
```

The dotted lines are produced by the VisiCalc command "/-", followed by the character to be used in the line. This command fills a cell with the chosen character regardless of the current (or subsequent) width of the cell. The cell must then be replicated across the sheet. So, to insert horizontal lines above and below the column headings, place the cursor on row 2 (i.e. the first heading row) and type /IR to insert a blank row. Now place the cursor in cell A2 (the left hand end of the blank row) and type /--. The /- will generate a cell full of – symbols. This cell must now be replicated along the rest of the row (use /R with source A2 and target range B2 to G2). Now insert a row at row 5, and repeat the line generation sequence again. Do the same for row 18. Now move the cursor to A20 and type /-=. This will generate a cell full of = symbols. Now replicate it across the rest of the sheet. Looks much better, doesn't it!

The worksheet's appearance can be improved further by slightly reducing the column widths. Unfortunately, while this is possible, what's done to one column automatically is done to the rest, so all column widths must be the same. (The extended version of VisiCalc overcomes this weakness.) Just out of curiosity, try increasing the column width to, perhaps, 12 characters. To do this type /GC12 and press return. Notice that the dotted lines still occupy the complete cell widths – as if they were made of elastic. Now shrink them to 6 characters wide (/GC6 return). You can see (fig.12) that the column headings have been truncated and that the totals in line 19 are displayed as ">>>>>". This indicates that the totals are too large to be displayed in the space allowed.

```
Fig.12   A     B     C     D     E     F     G
    1                          TAX RA 30
    2------------------------------------------
    3  EMP.  EMP.HOURLYHOURS  GROSS   TAX   NET
    4 NUMB. NAME  RATE WORKED   PAY   DUE   PAY
    5------------------------------------------
    6  0052 BROWN  1.50 37.20 55.80 16.74 39.06
    7  0098 GREEN  1.60 40.00 64.00 19.20 44.80
    8  0133 BLACK  1.95 36.50 71.18 21.35 49.82
    9  1432 WHITE  2.01 42.20 84.82 25.45 59.38
   10  1545 JONES  1.95 37.30 72.74 21.82 50.91
   11  2386 VANCE  1.95 28.00 54.60 16.38 38.22
   12  2912 EVANS  1.60 38.50 61.60 18.48 43.12
   13  3005 KING   1.50 39.40 59.10 17.73 41.37
   14  3112 BAKER  1.50 38.25 57.38 17.21 40.16
   15  3610 SMITH  1.60 29.70 47.52 14.26 33.26
   16                          0.00  0.00  0.00
   17                          0.00  0.00  0.00
   18------------------------------------------
   19      TOTALS       >>>>> >>>>> >>>>> >>>>>
   20==========================================
```

Now try widening the columns to 7 characters as in fig.13.

```
Fig.13     A      B      C      D      E      F      G
     1                             TAX RAT 30
     2-------------------------------------------------
     3   EMP.   EMP. HOURLY HOURS   GROSS    TAX    NET
     4  NUMB.   NAME   RATE WORKED    PAY    DUE    PAY
     5-------------------------------------------------
     6   0052  BROWN   1.50  37.20  55.80  16.74  39.06
     7   0098  GREEN   1.60  40.00  64.00  19.20  44.80
     8   0133  BLACK   1.95  36.50  71.18  21.35  49.82
     9   1432  WHITE   2.01  42.20  84.82  25.45  59.38
    10   1545  JONES   1.95  37.30  72.74  21.82  50.91
    11   2386  VANCE   1.95  28.00  54.60  16.38  38.22
    12   2912  EVANS   1.60  38.50  61.60  18.48  43.12
    13   3005   KING   1.50  39.40  59.10  17.73  41.37
    14   3112  BAKER   1.50  38.25  57.38  17.21  40.16
    15   3610  SMITH   1.60  29.70  47.52  14.26  33.26
    16                               0.00   0.00   0.00
    17                               0.00   0.00   0.00
    18-------------------------------------------------
    19        TOTALS        367.05 628.73 188.62 440.11
    20=================================================
```

Only the heading "TAX RATE%" still needs adjusting. Perhaps the best way to do this is to type "TAX" into cell D1. Then type " RATE %" into cell E1 and left justify cell E1. The result should look like fig.14.

```
Fig.14     A      B      C      D      E      F      G
     1                             TAX RATE % 30
     2-------------------------------------------------
     3   EMP.   EMP. HOURLY HOURS   GROSS    TAX    NET
     4  NUMB.   NAME   RATE WORKED    PAY    DUE    PAY
     5-------------------------------------------------
     6   0052  BROWN   1.50  37.20  55.80  16.74  39.06
     7   0098  GREEN   1.60  40.00  64.00  19.20  44.80
     8   0133  BLACK   1.95  36.50  71.18  21.35  49.82
     9   1432  WHITE   2.01  42.20  84.82  25.45  59.38
    10   1545  JONES   1.95  37.30  72.74  21.82  50.91
    11   2386  VANCE   1.95  28.00  54.60  16.38  38.22
    12   2912  EVANS   1.60  38.50  61.60  18.48  43.12
    13   3005   KING   1.50  39.40  59.10  17.73  41.37
    14   3112  BAKER   1.50  38.25  57.38  17.21  40.16
    15   3610  SMITH   1.60  29.70  47.52  14.26  33.26
    16                               0.00   0.00   0.00
    17                               0.00   0.00   0.00
    18-------------------------------------------------
    19        TOTALS        367.05 628.73 188.62 440.11
    20=================================================
```

It might be a good idea to save the sheet now just in case of accidents, perhaps as PAY14.

There are a few more useful functions that could conveniently be included here, such as @AVERAGE, Maximum (@MAX) and Minimum (@MIN). They are inserted into the worksheet in exactly the same way as for @SUM (i.e. @SUM(start range...end range)) and have the same format. After restoring the column width to 9 characters (/GC9), the worksheet now looks like fig.15.

Fig.15	A	B	C	D	E	F	G
1				TAX RATE % 30			
2	---------	---------	---------	---------	---------	---------	---------
3	EMP.	EMP.	HOURLY	HOURS	GROSS	TAX	NET
4	NUMB.	NAME	RATE	WORKED	PAY	DUE	PAY
5	---------	---------	---------	---------	---------	---------	---------
6	0052	BROWN	1.50	37.20	55.80	16.74	39.06
7	0098	GREEN	1.60	40.00	64.00	19.20	44.80
8	0133	BLACK	1.95	36.50	71.18	21.35	49.82
9	1432	WHITE	2.01	42.20	84.82	25.45	59.38
10	1545	JONES	1.95	37.30	72.74	21.82	50.91
11	2386	VANCE	1.95	28.00	54.60	16.38	38.22
12	2912	EVANS	1.60	38.50	61.60	18.48	43.12
13	3005	KING	1.50	39.40	59.10	17.73	41.37
14	3112	BAKER	1.50	38.25	57.38	17.21	40.16
15	3610	SMITH	1.60	29.70	47.52	14.26	33.26
16					0.00	0.00	0.00
17					0.00	0.00	0.00
18	---------	---------	---------	---------	---------	---------	---------
19		TOTALS		367.05	628.73	188.62	440.11
20		AVERAGE		36.71	52.39	15.72	36.68
21		MAXIMUM		42.20	84.82	25.45	59.39
22		MINIMUM		0	0	0	0
23	=========	=========	=========	=========	=========	=========	=========

It will be examined in some detail in the next chapter, so make sure you save this version of the worksheet now, perhaps as PAY15.

RECAP

/IR inserts a row at the cursor position.

/-- fills a cell with – symbols, and

/-= fills a cell with = symbols. Any character can be used instead of the - or =.

/R is used to replicate the – or = across the whole sheet.

/GCn will change all the column widths to n characters. Numbers too large for their cells will be displayed as 〉〉〉〉〉 instead. Making columns narrower may also damage the column headings. The cure is to widen the columns slightly until all is o.k.

@AVERAGE (range start...range end) will calculate the average of the values in the range.

@MAX (start...end) will find the largest value in the range.

@MIN (start...end) will find the smallest value.

7

Changing values and extending the sheet

It can take a lot of time and effort to set up a worksheet – perhaps almost as much as doing it by hand (once). However, recalculation of the sheet takes only a few seconds. For a really large sheet, it could take perhaps a minute or so, but manual recalculation of such a large sheet would almost certainly take at least a day!

Reload the worksheet saved (as PAY15) at the end of the previous chapter (if it's not already on the screen). Now try changing the tax rate in cell F1 and watch the effect. You'll have to concentrate closely on the screen in order to see what happens, since the recalculation takes place very quickly. Try changing the tax rate again and observe the effect. You should see the changes in the tax due and net pay columns rippling down them column by column. Now try changing the hours worked for each employee and observe the effects. Notice that the sheet is recalculated each time a change is made, and that there is a definite, though short, pause before a subsequent change can be made. If this were a very large sheet taking perhaps 15 seconds to recalculate, this would mean that only four changes could be made in each minute so that it would take at least two and a half minutes to key in the hours worked for our ten employees! To overcome this delay, it would be better to be able to type in all the changes to be made and then to initiate recalculation. The /GRM (Global, Recalculate, Manual) command switches off the automatic recalculation. Recalculation now only takes place when you type an exclamation mark (!). To switch back to automatic recalculation, type /GRA. Try switching to manual recalculation, making a few changes and then pressing "!".

Clear the worksheet (/C). (You DID save the sheet at the end of the previous chapter didn't you?) This is a rather drastic move so VisiCalc gives you a chance to retrieve the situation if you do not intend to clear the screen, merely by pressing return. Confirm you wish to clear the screen by pressing "Y", and reload the sheet (PAY15) saved at the end of the previous chapter. Now examine lines 19 to 22. The TOTALS, AVERAGE and MAXIMUM rows look correct, but the MINIMUM line looks wrong. Surely the minimum hours worked are 28, not zero? The explanation lies in the fact that the two blank entries in cells D16 and D17 are treated as if they contain zeroes when calculating anything except the average.

Extension of the worksheet to accommodate more employees is easy, but must be done with care. Blank rows must be inserted wherever necessary and the formulae replicated into them. However, care must be taken that the new rows still fall within the ranges specified for totalling etc. Insertion of a blank line below row 6 or above row 17 results in the totalling (etc) formulae being correctly amended, but inserting at row 6 will not. Try inserting a blank row at row 10, for example, and then examine the formula in cell D20 (it was D19 before the insertion). It's still correct. Now insert a blank row at row 6 and examine the formula now in D21. It's now incorrect. The best way of inserting rows into this sheet is to insert blank rows where necessary, below row 6, and then to replicate the formulae in row 17 (or 16) into each of the blank rows. Try the following. Clear the sheet and reload again the one saved (PAY15) at the end of the previous chapter. Insert three rows at row 16. Now replicate what was row 17 (and is now row 20) as follows: Type /R. The source range is A20 to G20 and the target range is A16 to A18. This results in the contents of range A20 to G20 being replicated into A16 to G16, A17 to G17 and A18 to G18, the formulae being adjusted as required, (all relative except F1).

Labels, so far as formulae are concerned, have arithmetic values of zero. Advantage can be taken of this fact to extend the ranges in the totalling, etc, calculations to start and end on the horizontal lines rather than on the first and last employees. Now a new employee can be inserted anywhere between the horizontal lines and not just before the last employee space. Try changing the totalling (etc.) formulae so that the range involved is horizontal line to horizontal line. Now insert a blank row immediately below the last employee name, and check the correctness of one of the formulae. Since a label has an arithmetic value of zero, the MINIMUM function still will not produce the correct answer, but the others will do so. The contents of a cell such as a label or formula can be altered using the editing command /E. A row can be deleted by placing the cursor anywhere on the row to be deleted and typing /DR. A column can be deleted in a similar fashion. Consult your VisiCalc manual for the details since they may vary from computer to computer.

Notice that recalculation takes place column by column. To change this to row by row, merely type /GOR (Global, Order, Row). To revert to column by column, use /GOC. A point to watch for when choosing the order of recalculation is that before using the value in a cell you must make sure that the value is the current correct one. If a formula in cell B2 (for example) needs a value in C3 (for example) which in turn depends on values elsewhere on the sheet, it is quite possible that on recalculation C3 will contain an out of date value and so B2 will also be incorrect. The correct value of C3 will not be calculated until after B2 has already been calculated! This is an example of "forward referencing". In this case it is immaterial whether the sheet is recalculated by rows or by columns. The cure in most cases is to recalculate the sheet twice. However, beware of possible errors going unnoticed. The following example illustrates forward referencing.

> Clear the VisiCalc worksheet using /C.
>
> Now type a number into cell A1. (Any number will do.) Into cell B2 type the formula +A1+C3. Into cell C3 type the formula +A1.
>
> Now change the value of A1 (try zero). The answer is wrong.
>
> Now press "!". The answer is now correct.
>
> Now change the order of calculation (/GOR) and try again. There's no difference, is there?
>
> Now change the formula in cell C3 to +A1+B2 and see what happens.

The latter is known as a "circular reference" and ought to be avoided at all costs, since the worksheet can never be correct.

RECAP

/GOR sets recalculation order to "row by row".

/GOC sets recalculation order to "column by column".

/GRM switches off automatic recalculation.

/GRA switches it back on again.

! initiates recalculation.

/R can be used to replicate a whole row (or column) into a range of other rows (or columns).

/I can be used to insert blank rows which will be included in the range of cells totalled by @SUM (etc.) provided the blank rows are inserted at (or below) the row which is the start of the range. If the range includes a row containing a label, then the label will have an arithmetic value of zero. If the range boundaries are cells containing labels, then insertions may be made anywhere between the labels and the ranges will be adjusted correctly. /I can be used in a similar fashion to insert columns.

/DR deletes the row containing the cursor.

/DC deletes the column containing the cursor.

/C clears the whole sheet.

/E allows the contents of the current cell to be edited. (See your VisiCalc manual for details.)

Forward references involve using a cell in a calculation when this cell has not yet been recalculated correctly. Forcing another recalculation using "!" usually produces the correct results.

Circular references involve a circular trail of mutually dependent formulae. Definitely to be avoided at all costs!

8

Table lookups

Clear the worksheet and reload the sheet saved at the end of chapter six (PAY15). It should look like this:

```
Fig.16     A         B         C         D         E         F         G
  1                                     TAX     RATE % 30
  2----------------------------------------------------------------------
  3       EMP.      EMP.    HOURLY    HOURS     GROSS       TAX       NET
  4      NUMB.      NAME      RATE   WORKED       PAY       DUE       PAY
  5----------------------------------------------------------------------
  6       0052     BROWN      1.50    37.20     55.80     16.74     39.06
  7       0098     GREEN      1.60    40.00     64.00     19.20     44.80
  8       0133     BLACK      1.95    36.50     71.18     21.35     49.82
  9       1432     WHITE      2.01    42.20     84.82     25.45     59.38
 10       1545     JONES      1.95    37.30     72.74     21.82     50.91
 11       2386     VANCE      1.95    28.00     54.60     16.38     38.22
 12       2912     EVANS      1.60    38.50     61.60     18.48     43.12
 13       3005      KING      1.50    39.40     59.10     17.73     41.37
 14       3112     BAKER      1.50    38.25     57.38     17.21     40.16
 15       3610     SMITH      1.60    29.70     47.52     14.26     33.26
 16                                              0.00      0.00      0.00
 17                                              0.00      0.00      0.00
 18----------------------------------------------------------------------
 19                TOTALS            367.05    628.73    188.62    440.11
 20               AVERAGE             36.71     52.39     15.72     36.68
 21               MAXIMUM             42.20     84.82     25.45     59.39
 22               MINIMUM                 0         0         0         0
 23======================================================================
```

If there were a large number of employees, changing all the hourly rates would involve considerable work. Normally, however, there are relatively few different pay rates, so it would be much simpler if we could give each employee a job group number and examine a table of hourly rates using this job group number. There are two VisiCalc functions which are of use in these circumstances – @CHOOSE and @LOOKUP. We'll consider the use of @CHOOSE first.

The format of @CHOOSE is

```
@CHOOSE(number N,start of table...end of table)
```

and chooses the Nth number in the specified table. This means, in effect, that N must lie in the range 1,2,3 etc., so that the first, second, third, etc entry from the table can be chosen. Try making the following changes to the worksheet:

Set the column width to 7 characters, insert a blank column at C, head it "JOB GROUP" and add the horizontal lines. In rows 6 to 15 type in the job groups as in the example in fig.17 below. Now type in the heading and hourly rates in rows 26 to 32 in column B. Instead of the hourly rates (now in column D) type

```
@CHOOSE(C6,B28...B32)
```

into cell D6 and replicate this formula down to row 17. Recalculate the sheet if it's in manual mode. The hourly rates should appear exactly as before, but they have been chosen from a table rather than having been typed in individually.

```
Fig.17  A       B       C       D       E       F       G
 1                                      TAX RATE % 30
 2--------------------------------------------------------
 3     EMP.    EMP.     JOB HOURLY  HOURS   GROSS     TAX
 4    NUMB.    NAME   GROUP   RATE WORKED     PAY     DUE
 5--------------------------------------------------------
 6     0052   BROWN       1   1.50  37.20   55.80   16.74
 7     0098   GREEN       2   1.60  40.00   64.00   19.20
 8     0133   BLACK       3   1.95  36.50   71.18   21.35
 9     1432   WHITE       4   2.01  42.20   84.82   25.45
10     1545   JONES       3   1.95  37.30   72.74   21.82
11     2386   VANCE       3   1.95  28.00   54.60   16.38
12     2912   EVANS       2   1.60  38.50   61.60   18.48
13     3005    KING       1   1.50  39.40   59.10   17.73
14     3112   BAKER       1   1.50  38.25   57.38   17.21
15     3610   SMITH       2   1.60  29.70   47.52   14.26
16                              NA             NA      NA
17                              NA             NA      NA
18--------------------------------------------------------
19           TOTALS                   367.05   NA      NA
20          AVERAGE                    36.71   NA      NA
21          MAXIMUM                    42.20   NA      NA
22          MINIMUM                        0   NA      NA
23========================================================
24
25
26          RATE/HR
27          -------
28             1.50
29             1.60
30             1.95
31             2.01
32             2.43
33
```

The "NA" entries mean "not applicable" and are a result of the @CHOOSE function attempting to choose the "zeroth" entry in the rate/hour table. Deleting rows 16 and 17 will cure this error, but may cause another error! Delete these two rows and examine the result. It should look like fig.18.

```
Fig.18    A        B        C        D        E        F        G        H
   1                                        TAX RATE % 30
   2---------------------------------------------------------------------
   3    EMP.     EMP.      JOB  HOURLY  HOURS      GROSS      TAX      NET
   4   NUMB.     NAME    GROUP    RATE  WORKED       PAY      DUE      PAY
   5---------------------------------------------------------------------
   6    0052    BROWN        1    1.50   37.20     55.80    16.74    39.06
   7    0098    GREEN        2    1.60   40.00     64.00    19.20    44.80
   8    0133    BLACK        3    1.95   36.50     71.18    21.35    49.82
   9    1432    WHITE        4    2.01   42.20     84.82    25.45    59.38
  10    1545    JONES        3    1.95   37.30     72.74    21.82    50.91
  11    2386    VANCE        3    1.95   28.00     54.60    16.38    38.22
  12    2912    EVANS        2    1.60   38.50     61.60    18.48    43.12
  13    3005     KING        1    1.50   39.40     59.10    17.73    41.37
  14    3112    BAKER        1    1.50   38.25     57.38    17.21    40.16
  15    3610    SMITH        2    1.60   29.70     47.52    14.26    33.26
  16---------------------------------------------------------------------
  17           TOTALS                    ERROR     ERROR    ERROR    ERROR
  18          AVERAGE                    ERROR     ERROR    ERROR    ERROR
  19          MAXIMUM                    ERROR     ERROR    ERROR    ERROR
  20          MINIMUM                    ERROR     ERROR    ERROR    ERROR
  21=====================================================================
  22
  23
  24          RATE/HR
  25          -------
  26             1.50
  27             1.60
  28             1.95
  29             2.01
  30             2.43
  31
```

Now place the cursor on one of the cells containing "ERROR", and examine the formula. Deleting row 17 also deleted all references to row 17 and thus damaged this formula. After repairing the damaged formulae, recalculate the sheet. It should now look like fig.19.

```
Fig.19   A       B       C      D       E       F       G       H
    1                                   TAX RATE % 30
    2-----------------------------------------------------------------
    3   EMP.    EMP.     JOB HOURLY HOURS    GROSS     TAX     NET
    4  NUMB.    NAME   GROUP   RATE WORKED     PAY     DUE     PAY
    5-----------------------------------------------------------------
    6   0052   BROWN       1   1.50  37.20   55.80   16.74   39.06
    7   0098   GREEN       2   1.60  40.00   64.00   19.20   44.80
    8   0133   BLACK       3   1.95  36.50   71.18   21.35   49.82
    9   1432   WHITE       4   2.01  42.20   84.82   25.45   59.38
   10   1545   JONES       3   1.95  37.30   72.74   21.82   50.91
   11   2386   VANCE       3   1.95  28.00   54.60   16.38   38.22
   12   2912   EVANS       2   1.60  38.50   61.60   18.48   43.12
   13   3005    KING       1   1.50  39.40   59.10   17.73   41.37
   14   3112   BAKER       1   1.50  38.25   57.38   17.21   40.16
   15   3610   SMITH       2   1.60  29.70   47.52   14.26   33.26
   16-----------------------------------------------------------------
   17         TOTALS                367.05  628.73  188.62  440.11
   18        AVERAGE                 36.71   62.87   18.86   44.01
   19        MAXIMUM                 42.20   84.82   25.45   59.38
   20        MINIMUM                 28.00   47.52   14.26   33.26
   21=================================================================
   22
   23
   24        RATE/HR
   25        -------
   26           1.50
   27           1.60
   28           1.95
   29           2.01
   30           2.43
   31
```

Now save this version of your worksheet (as PAY19).

@CHOOSE picks the Nth entry from a table. If N is a large number, then the table must also be large, since it must start at entry number 1 and continue with entry number 2, 3, 4 and so on up to at least N. If the job groups are grouped so that all job group numbers (say) in the range 1 to 9 are paid at the same rate, all the jobs from 10 to 19 at another rate and so on, then @CHOOSE becomes rather cumbersome. An alternative would be to use @LOOKUP. The @LOOKUP function takes the same form as @CHOOSE, i.e.

```
@LOOKUP(N,start of table...end of table)
```

and works by scanning the job group column in Fig.20 until an entry is found which is larger than the individual employee's job group. The rate per hour alongside the entry immediately before this is the correct hourly rate.

```
Fig.20    A        B        C       D      E        F       G       H
     1                                    TAX RATE % 30
     2--------------------------------------------------------------------
     3    EMP.     EMP.     JOB  HOURLY  HOURS    GROSS     TAX     NET
     4   NUMB.     NAME   GROUP    RATE  WORKED     PAY     DUE     PAY
     5--------------------------------------------------------------------
     6    0052   BROWN        1    1.50   37.20   55.80   16.74   39.06
     7    0098   GREEN        2    1.60   40.00   64.00   19.20   44.80
     8    0133   BLACK        3    1.95   36.50   71.18   21.35   49.82
     9    1432   WHITE        4    2.01   42.20   84.82   25.45   59.38
    10    1545   JONES        3    1.95   37.30   72.74   21.82   50.91
    11    2386   VANCE        3    1.95   28.00   54.60   16.38   38.22
    12    2912   EVANS        2    1.60   38.50   61.60   18.48   43.12
    13    3005    KING        1    1.50   39.40   59.10   17.73   41.37
    14    3112   BAKER        1    1.50   38.25   57.38   17.21   40.16
    15    3610   SMITH        2    1.60   29.70   47.52   14.26   33.26
    16--------------------------------------------------------------------
    17            TOTALS                 367.05  628.73  188.62  440.11
    18           AVERAGE                  36.71   62.87   18.86   44.01
    19           MAXIMUM                  42.20   84.82   25.45   59.38
    20           MINIMUM                  28.00   47.52   14.26   33.26
    21====================================================================
    22
    23
    24 JOB GP RATE/HR
    25 --------------
    26        1   1.50
    27        2   1.60
    28        3   1.95
    29        4   2.01
    30        5   2.43
    31
```

Save this worksheet (as PAY20).

Now try changing the job groups in rows 26 to 30 to 10,20,30,40 & 50, and change those in column C to numbers similar to those in Fig.21. Recalculate the sheet and note that the results are the same as before. The hourly rate of 1.50 applies to all job groups up to, but not including, 20. The rate of 1.60 applies to job groups from 20 up to, but not including, 30, and so on.

The sheet should look something like fig.21.

```
Fig.21   A       B       C       D       E       F       G       H
 1                                       TAX RATE % 30
 2---------------------------------------------------------------
 3    EMP.    EMP.     JOB HOURLY HOURS     GROSS     TAX     NET
 4   NUMB.    NAME   GROUP   RATE WORKED      PAY     DUE     PAY
 5---------------------------------------------------------------
 6    0052  BROWN        1   1.50  37.20    55.80   16.74   39.06
 7    0098  GREEN        2   1.60  40.00    64.00   19.20   44.80
 8    0133  BLACK        3   1.95  36.50    71.18   21.35   49.82
 9    1432  WHITE        4   2.01  42.20    84.82   25.45   59.38
10    1545  JONES        3   1.95  37.30    72.74   21.82   50.91
11    2386  VANCE        3   1.95  28.00    54.60   16.38   38.22
12    2912  EVANS        2   1.60  38.50    61.60   18.48   43.12
13    3005   KING        1   1.50  39.40    59.10   17.73   41.37
14    3112  BAKER        1   1.50  38.25    57.38   17.21   40.16
15    3610  SMITH        2   1.60  29.70    47.52   14.26   33.26
16---------------------------------------------------------------
17            TOTALS               367.05   628.73  188.62  440.11
18           AVERAGE                36.71    62.87   18.86   44.01
19           MAXIMUM                42.20    84.82   25.45   59.38
20           MINIMUM                28.00    47.52   14.26   33.26
21===============================================================
22
23
24 JOB GP RATE/HR
25 --------------
26       0    1.50
27      20    1.60
28      30    1.95
29      40    2.01
30      50    2.43
31
```

RECAP

@CHOOSE (N,start of table...end of table) picks the Nth entry from a table specified by "start" and "end".

@LOOKUP (N,start...end) scans the table specified by "start" and "end" until an entry larger than N is found. The entry in the column adjacent to the immediately preceding entry in the table is the desired value.

/D (DELETE row or column) injudiciously used can wreck existing formulae if either the start or end rows (or columns) of a range are involved.

9

If...

Load the worksheet saved in the previous chapter (PAY20). It should look something like this:

```
Fig.22    A       B       C       D       E       F       G       H
   1                                   TAX RATE % 30
   2---------------------------------------------------------------
   3   EMP.    EMP.     JOB HOURLY  HOURS   GROSS     TAX     NET
   4  NUMB.    NAME   GROUP   RATE WORKED     PAY     DUE     PAY
   5---------------------------------------------------------------
   6   0052   BROWN       1   1.50  37.20   55.80   16.74   39.06
   7   0098   GREEN       2   1.60  40.00   64.00   19.20   44.80
   8   0133   BLACK       3   1.95  36.50   71.18   21.35   49.82
   9   1432   WHITE       4   2.01  42.20   84.82   25.45   59.38
  10   1545   JONES       3   1.95  37.30   72.74   21.82   50.91
  11   2386   VANCE       3   1.95  28.00   54.60   16.38   38.22
  12   2912   EVANS       2   1.60  38.50   61.60   18.48   43.12
  13   3005    KING       1   1.50  39.40   59.10   17.73   41.37
  14   3112   BAKER       1   1.50  38.25   57.38   17.21   40.16
  15   3610   SMITH       2   1.60  29.70   47.52   14.26   33.26
  16---------------------------------------------------------------
  17         TOTALS                367.05  628.73  188.62  440.11
  18        AVERAGE                 36.71   62.87   18.86   44.01
  19        MAXIMUM                 42.20   84.82   25.45   59.38
  20        MINIMUM                 28.00   47.52   14.26   33.26
  21===============================================================
  22
  23
  24 JOB GP RATE/HR
  25---------------
  26       1   1.50
  27       2   1.60
  28       3   1.95
  29       4   2.01
  30       5   2.43
  31
```

To make the tax calculation a shade more realistic, tax allowances should be taken into account. To do this, insert a column for "TAX CODE" at column D and enter the tax codes shown in fig.23. At what is now column H, insert a column headed "FREE PAY". The formula for this is merely (tax code * 10) / 52 – assuming a 52 week year. The taxable pay is gross pay minus free pay, and so the tax due is this taxable pay times the tax rate (%)/ 100. However, tax due cannot be a negative amount (refunds are not catered for here), so the tax due must be either a positive sum or zero. The formula for this is

```
    @IF((gross pay – free pay > 0),(gross
pay – free pay)*tax rate/100,0).
```

Translated, this means:

> If gross pay – free pay is greater than zero
> then put (gross pay – free pay)*tax rate/100
> into the cell
> else put zero in the cell.

Type this formula into cell I6 and replicate it down the column. Recalculate, if necessary. This is what you should have:

```
Fig.23  A       B       C       D       E       F       G       H       I       J
   1                                                    TAX RATE % 30
   2------------------------------------------------------------------------------
   3   EMP.    EMP.     JOB     TAX  HOURLY  HOURS   GROSS    FREE     TAX     NET
   4  NUMB.    NAME   GROUP    CODE    RATE WORKED     PAY     PAY     DUE     PAY
   5------------------------------------------------------------------------------
   6   0052   BROWN       1     193    1.50  37.20   55.80   37.12    5.61   50.19
   7   0098   GREEN       2     240    1.60  40.00   64.00   46.15    5.35   58.65
   8   0133   BLACK       3     432    1.95  36.50   71.18   83.08    0.00   71.18
   9   1432   WHITE       4     278    2.01  42.20   84.82   53.46    9.41   75.41
  10   1545   JONES       3     345    1.95  37.30   72.74   66.35    1.92   70.82
  11   2386   VANCE       3     654    1.95  28.00   54.60  125.77    0.00   54.60
  12   2912   EVANS       2     231    1.60  38.50   61.60   44.42    5.15   56.45
  13   3005    KING       1     510    1.50  39.40   59.10   98.08    0.00   59.10
  14   3112   BAKER       1     488    1.50  38.25   57.38   93.85    0.00   57.38
  15   3610   SMITH       2     325    1.60  29.70   47.52   62.50    0.00   47.52
  16------------------------------------------------------------------------------
  17         TOTALS                             367.05  628.73  710.77   27.44  601.29
  18        AVERAGE                              36.71   62.87   71.08    2.74   60.13
  19        MAXIMUM                              42.20   84.82  125.77    9.41   75.41
  20        MINIMUM                              28.00   47.52   37.12    0.00   47.52
  21==============================================================================
  22
  23
  24  JOB GP RATE/HR
  25  --------------
  26       1    1.50
  27       2    1.60
  28       3    1.95
  29       4    2.01
  30       5    2.43
  31
```

(The heading "TAX RATE %" on row 1 has been shifted along a column.) Note that where free pay is greater than gross pay then the tax due is zero. Now save this sheet (as PAY23).

@IF can also be used to indicate whether a particular condition is true or false. For example, to indicate for each employee, whether that employee has net pay of £55 or greater, the formula

`@IF(J6>=55,@TRUE,@FALSE)` could be entered into K6 and

replicated down the column. The result would look like this:

```
Fig.24   A        B       C       D       E       F       G       H       I       J       K
   1                                                    TAX RATE % 30
   2----------------------------------------------------------------------------------------
   3   EMP.     EMP.     JOB     TAX  HOURLY   HOURS   GROSS    FREE    TAX     NET  >=55?
   4  NUMB.     NAME   GROUP    CODE    RATE  WORKED     PAY     PAY    DUE     PAY
   5----------------------------------------------------------------------------------------
   6   0052    BROWN       1     193    1.50   37.20   55.80   37.12   5.61   50.19   FALSE
   7   0098    GREEN       2     240    1.60   40.00   64.00   46.15   5.35   58.65    TRUE
   8   0133    BLACK       3     432    1.95   36.50   71.18   83.08   0.00   71.18    TRUE
   9   1432    WHITE       4     278    2.01   42.20   84.82   53.46   9.41   75.41    TRUE
  10   1545    JONES       3     345    1.95   37.30   72.74   66.35   1.92   70.82    TRUE
  11   2386    VANCE       3     654    1.95   28.00   54.60  125.77   0.00   54.60   FALSE
  12   2912    EVANS       2     231    1.60   38.50   61.60   44.42   5.15   56.45    TRUE
  13   3005     KING       1     510    1.50   39.40   59.10   98.08   0.00   59.10    TRUE
  14   3112    BAKER       1     488    1.50   38.25   57.38   93.85   0.00   57.38    TRUE
  15   3610    SMITH       2     325    1.60   29.70   47.52   62.50   0.00   47.52   FALSE
  16----------------------------------------------------------------------------------------
  17          TOTALS                          367.05  628.73  710.77  27.44  601.29
  18         AVERAGE                           36.71   62.87   71.08   2.74   60.13
  19         MAXIMUM                           42.20   84.82  125.77   9.41   75.41
  20         MINIMUM                           28.00   47.52   37.12   0.00   47.52
  21========================================================================================
  22
  23
  24  JOB GP RATE/HR
  25  --------------
  26       1    1.50
  27       2    1.60
  28       3    1.95
  29       4    2.01
  30       5    2.43
  31
  32
```

RECAP

@IF(test, action if true,action if false) can be used to choose between alternative courses of action. These can result in either of two calculation formulae being used, or can result in the display of TRUE or FALSE instead of values.

Although not mentioned in this chapter, it is also possible to test whether the word "ERROR" appears in a cell and to take certain action if it does, and other action if it doesn't. In this case, the form is

`@IF( @ISERROR, action if true, action if false).`

10

Printing the worksheet

Most printers can print up to either 80 characters or 132 characters per line. Normally, 80 characters per line is the norm and anything else requires a special series of characters called a "set up string" to be sent to the printer before printing of the worksheet starts. VisiCalc does not check that the length of each line sent to the printer will fit onto the paper – that's your responsibility. The set up string required to cajole each printer into printing a non-standard line length varies from printer to printer, so you will have to consult the manual appropriate to your printer to ascertain the correct codes. Some printers provide a line feed when they receive a carriage return from VisiCalc, in addition to the line feed that VisiCalc also sends, and some require an extra line feed from VisiCalc since line-feed-plus-carriage-return is treated by these printers as if they were a carriage return on its own! Perforce, in this book we will have to deal with printers which produce 80 characters per line as standard, and do not produce an extra line feed. However, once VisiCalc has sent the printer command ("set up string") which switches off the extra line feed the first time, there is no need to repeat the command unless the printer is switched off, or some other set up string is sent which turns the extra line feed back on again.

To produce printed output, work out how many columns can be printed using an 80 character line. If you have used the default column width of nine characters, this will be eight columns (with a few characters per line left over). Any other column width, of course, may allow a different number of columns to be printed. However, no matter how many columns are to be printed, the principle is the same. The part of the worksheet to be printed must be rectangular in shape and this rectangle is outlined by specifying the top left hand corner and the bottom right hand corner. Everything within this rectangle will be printed. A good guide as to whether it will fit on the paper is that if it fits on an 80 column screen, it'll go on the paper. It it fits within two 40 column screens, then it will also fit onto the paper.

So, to start printing, first place the cursor on the cell which will be the top left hand corner of the printout. Type /PP if your printer is in slot 1, or /P followed by the slot number if your printer is in any other slot. Follow this with the (optional) set up string then the co-ordinates of the bottom right hand corner cell. These co-ordinates may either be typed or the cursor may be moved to the bottom right cell instead. Now press return and printing should commence. If it doesn't, check that the printer is switched on at the mains and that any print enable switch is also set at "on". To cancel printing at any point, press CTRL-C (i.e. hold down the control key and press C at the same time). If the line to be printed is too long, most printers will "wrap around" and print the overlong part on the next line, which makes rather a mess of the printout. The set up string may require the use of ESC and CTRL sequences which cannot be typed directly. In these cases, CTRL-C is simulated by pressing SHIFT-N followed by C, and CTRL-E by SHIFT-N followed by E.

It is also possible to store on floppy disk (using /PF), for use elsewhere, what would otherwise have been printed. In fact, the draft of this book was typed using a word processing programme. The VisiCalc printouts were stored on disk and then incorporated into the text without actually printing them out on paper from VisiCalc.

It may be that the worksheet as displayed on the screen is not suitable for printing directly, perhaps because there is irrelevant or sensitive information embedded within the information to be printed. Before printing part of the worksheet, these columns (or rows) can be moved out of the way to leave a printable part of the sheet. To move a column (or row), first ensure that re-calculation will be manually controlled (/GRM), place the cursor on the column (or row) to be moved and type /M. Now specify the new column and same row number (or new row and same column number) to which the column (or row) is to be moved. The columns (or rows) which are displaced are shifted one column to the right (or one row down) and any formulae involved are adjusted to suit their new columns (or rows). Try this by re-loading the worksheet saved in chapter nine as PAY23. Now move columns A and B to just before column E as follows. Switch off automatic re-calculation by typing /GRM. Now place the cursor on cell A6, type /M, and then type E6. Column A will become column D. What was column B will now be column A. Now repeat this to move what is now column A again to become column E. The result should look something like fig.25.

Fig.25	A	B	C	D	E	F	G	H	I	J
1							TAX	RATE % 30		
2	--------	--------	--------	--------	--------	--------	--------	--------	--------	--------
3	JOB	TAX	EMP.	EMP.	HOURLY	HOURS	GROSS	FREE	TAX	NET
4	GROUP	CODE	NUMB.	NAME	RATE	WORKED	PAY	PAY	DUE	PAY
5	--------	--------	--------	--------	--------	--------	--------	--------	--------	--------
6	1	193	0052	BROWN	1.50	37.20	55.80	37.12	5.61	50.19
7	2	240	0098	GREEN	1.60	40.00	64.00	46.15	5.35	58.65
8	3	432	0133	BLACK	1.95	36.50	71.18	83.08	0.00	71.18
9	4	278	1432	WHITE	2.01	42.20	84.82	53.46	9.41	75.41
10	3	345	1545	JONES	1.95	37.30	72.74	66.35	1.92	70.82
11	3	654	2386	VANCE	1.95	28.00	54.60	125.77	0.00	54.60
12	2	231	2912	EVANS	1.60	38.50	61.60	44.42	5.15	56.45
13	1	510	3005	KING	1.50	39.40	59.10	98.08	0.00	59.10
14	1	488	3112	BAKER	1.50	38.25	57.38	93.85	0.00	57.38
15	2	325	3610	SMITH	1.60	29.70	47.52	62.50	0.00	47.52
16	--------	--------	--------	--------	--------	--------	--------	--------	--------	--------
17				TOTALS		367.05	628.73	710.77	27.44	601.29
18				AVERAGE		36.71	62.87	71.08	2.74	60.13
19				MAXIMUM		42.20	84.82	125.77	9.41	75.41
20				MINIMUM		28.00	47.52	37.12	0.00	47.52
21	========	========	========	========	========	========	========	========	========	========
22										
23										
24			JOB GP	RATE/HR						
25			--------	--------						
26			1	1.50						
27			2	1.60						
28			3	1.95						
29			4	2.01						
30			5	2.43						
31										

Note that not only have the employee numbers and employee names been moved, but also the job groups and rates/hour in rows 24 to 30.

Now place the cursor on cell C1, and type /PP followed by J21 to print the part of the sheet bounded by columns C and J and rows 1 and 21.

RECAP

/M is used to move a column (or row) to a position just before (or just above) the target column (or row). Any formulae involved in the move are adjusted to reflect the cells' new positions.

/P is used to initiate printing of a selected part of the worksheet. The part chosen is indicated by the co-ordinates of the top left-hand and bottom right-hand corners of the rectangular section of the worksheet to be printed. The printout may be directed to the printer (using /PP) or may be stored on disk for subsequent use by a word processor (using /PF). A line length of 80 characters is assumed unless a set up string is sent to the printer to indicate to it that longer lines, usually up to a maximum of 132 characters, will be sent. To accomodate 132 characters on eight-inch wide printer paper means that a compressed character set of 16.5 characters to an inch, rather than the standard 10 characters per inch, must be employed. The control characters needed from VisiCalc to tell the printer to print in a non-standard manner vary considerably from printer to printer. Consult the manual for your printer for these codes. The CTRL and ESC keys in a set up string are represented by SHIFT-N followed by C or E as appropriate.

11

Fixing calculated values and headings and splitting the screen

Suppose we wish to retain each week's total hours worked and total gross pay in a table at the end of the payroll as a summary. To insert the total hours and total gross pay into the correct week of the summary merely involves comparing the current week number (cell G22) with the week numbers in column E row 27 (etc.). If the week numbers match then the appropriate totals are placed in the cells in columns F and G on the same row. Otherwise zero is placed in these cells. Reload PAY23 and make these additions. This will produce something like fig. 26.

Fig.26	A	B	C	D	E	F	G	H	I	J
1							TAX	RATE % 30		
2	------	------	------	------	------	------	------	------	------	------
3	EMP.	EMP.	JOB	TAX	HOURLY	HOURS	GROSS	FREE	TAX	NET
4	NUMB.	NAME	GROUP	CODE	RATE	WORKED	PAY	PAY	DUE	PAY
5	------	------	------	------	------	------	------	------	------	------
6	0052	BROWN	1	193	1.50	37.20	55.80	37.12	5.61	50.19
7	0098	GREEN	2	240	1.60	40.00	64.00	46.15	5.35	58.65
8	0133	BLACK	3	432	1.95	36.50	71.18	83.08	0.00	71.18
9	1432	WHITE	4	278	2.01	42.20	84.82	53.46	9.41	75.41
10	1545	JONES	3	345	1.95	37.30	72.74	66.35	1.92	70.82
11	2386	VANCE	3	654	1.95	28.00	54.60	125.77	0.00	54.60
12	2912	EVANS	2	231	1.60	38.50	61.60	44.42	5.15	56.45
13	3005	KING	1	510	1.50	39.40	59.10	98.08	0.00	59.10
14	3112	BAKER	1	488	1.50	38.25	57.38	93.85	0.00	57.38
15	3610	SMITH	2	325	1.60	29.70	47.52	62.50	0.00	47.52
16	------	------	------	------	------	------	------	------	------	------
17		TOTALS				367.05	628.73	710.77	27.44	601.29
18		AVERAGE				36.71	62.87	71.08	2.74	60.13
19		MAXIMUM				42.20	84.82	125.77	9.41	75.41
20		MINIMUM				28.00	47.52	37.12	0.00	47.52
21	======	======	======	======	======	======	======	======	======	======
22					CURRENT	WEEK NO 1				
23						TOTAL	TOTAL			
24	JOB GP	RATE/HR				HOURS	GROSS			
25	------	------			WEEK	WORKED	PAY			
26	1	1.50			------	------	------			
27	2	1.60			1	367.05	628.73			
28	3	1.95			2	0	0			
29	4	2.01			3	0	0			
30	5	2.43			4	0	0			
31					5	0	0			
32					6	0	0			
33					7	0	0			
34					8	0	0			
35					9	0	0			
36					10	0	0			

Now change the week number in G22 and recalculate the sheet. The totals will now appear in row 28, and row 27 (week 1) will now contain zeroes since the formula in F27 is @IF(E27=G22,F17,0). The cure is startlingly simple. After calculating the values for a particular week, (for example week 1) place the cursor on each of the totals for that week (for example F27 and F28) and press # followed by "return". This will fix the calculated values and wipe out the formulae that calculated them. Now change the week number in cell G22 and recalculate the sheet. Note that the values already in columns F and G are not affected. In this way, historical figures may be preserved against change.

When scrolling the sheet to view cells lower down it can be a nuisance that the column headings disappear from view. To fix the headings so that only the sheet below them scrolls, place the cursor on the lowest row you wish to fix and type /TH. Now scroll the sheet vertically. The column headings stay put while the rest of the sheet scrolls up and down. Similarly, row labels may be fixed by placing the cursor on the leftmost column to be fixed and then typing /TV. Both column headings and row labels may be fixed in one go by placing the cursor on the cell which is both on the lowest row to be fixed and on the rightmost column to be fixed, and then typing /TB. All title fixes may be removed using /TN. Rows and columns fixed using /T can be entered only by using "goto" (⟩), so, since the cursor cannot be placed in these cells by means of the cursor control keys, the contents of such cells can be protected against accidental change.

The current screen represents a window on the worksheet. This window can be split into two smaller windows, either horizontally or vertically. To split the screen into two roughly equal parts, place the cursor in the centre of the screen and type /WH for a horizontal split, or /WV for a vertical split. The resulting two windows on the sheet can be scrolled independently or they may be locked in step with one another by typing /WS. Typing /WU unlocks them and allows them to be scrolled independently again. Each window may be set to a different column width. To move the cursor between windows, type ";". Splitting the screen allows you to compare the figures in parts of the sheet that otherwise could not be displayed together on the screen because of their distance apart in the worksheet. The split can be cancelled using /W1.

RECAP

#	fixes the value currently displayed in a cell and destroys any formulae used to calculate the value. It can be used to preserve historical figures.
/TH	fixes all rows from the cursor to the top of the screen against scrolling. It is usually used to ensure column headings are always present. The cursor cannot be placed into a cell which has been fixed using /T by means of the cursor control keys - "⟩" (goto) must be used instead.
/TV	fixes all columns from the cursor to its left.
/TB	combines /TH and /TV.
/TN	removes all title fixing.
/WH	splits the window into two windows, horizontally at the cursor position. Each window may be set to different column widths.
/WV	splits the window vertically at the cursor position.
/WS	synchronises scrolling of the two windows.
/WU	de-synchronises scrolling, allowing the windows to be scrolled independently.
/W1	removes the split and restores the single window.
;	transfers the cursor to the other window.

12

DIF files

"DIF" means "data interchange format" and DIF files are a means of storing the labels and values (but not the formulae) appearing in all or part of a worksheet so that they may be called back and used either in another part of the same worksheet or in an entirely separate worksheet. It is also possible to use them to pass labels and values to programs other than VisiCalc, such as plotting programs etc. Only their use within VisiCalc will be demonstrated here, however.

Suppose, in our payroll example, we wished to add a year-to-date gross pay column K. Calculating the new year-to-date figure for each week involves adding the current week's gross pay to last week's year-to-date figure. The obvious way to do this, you might think, is to place the formula +K6+G6 in cell K6. This will add Brown's gross pay to his year-to-date gross pay to give the new value. Indeed, it does just that – every time the sheet is recalculated! Try it and see. So if a mistake is made in entering any of the data and the sheet is re-calculated for the first time before the mistake is spotted, the re-calculation involved in correcting the mistake will make nonsense of the year-to-date figures. Try pressing "!" to test this out.

An alternative method is to have two year-to-date gross pay columns, one containing the figures as of last week, and the other containing the figures to be carried forward to next week. The gross pay for this week is added to last week's year-to-date gross pay to give next week's year-to-date figures. In the following, use the worksheet as in the middle of chapter 9 (PAY23) or re-load the worksheet saved in chapter 8 (PAY20). Now add the column headings (etc.) for columns K to N as in fig.27. The formula needed in cell M6 is +K6+G6, and that in N6 is +L6+I6. Format M6 and N6 and replicate these formulae down columns M and N, format columns K and L and recalculate the sheet. It should look something like fig. 27:

Fig.27	A	B	C	D	E	F	G	H	I	J	K	L	M	N
1							TAX RATE % 30							
2											OLD YEAR-T-D		NEW YEAR-T-D	
3	EMP.	EMP.	JOB	TAX	HOURLY	HOURS	GROSS	FREE	TAX	NET	GROSS	TAX	GROSS	TAX
4	NUMB.	NAME	GROUP	CODE	RATE	WORKED	PAY	PAY	DUE	PAY	PAY	PAID	PAY	PAID
5														
6	0052	BROWN	1	193	1.50	37.20	55.80	37.12	5.61	50.19			55.80	5.61
7	0098	GREEN	2	240	1.60	40.00	64.00	46.15	5.35	58.65			64.00	5.35
8	0133	BLACK	3	432	1.95	36.50	71.18	83.08	0.00	71.18			71.18	0.00
9	1432	WHITE	4	278	2.01	42.20	84.82	53.46	9.41	75.41			84.82	9.41
10	1545	JONES	3	345	1.95	37.30	72.74	66.35	1.92	70.82			72.74	1.92
11	2386	VANCE	3	654	1.95	28.00	54.60	125.77	0.00	54.60			54.60	0.00
12	2912	EVANS	2	231	1.60	38.50	61.60	44.42	5.15	56.45			61.60	5.15
13	3005	KING	1	510	1.50	39.40	59.10	98.08	0.00	59.10			59.10	0.00
14	3112	BAKER	1	488	1.50	38.25	57.38	93.85	0.00	57.38			57.38	0.00
15	3610	SMITH	2	325	1.60	29.70	47.52	62.50	0.00	47.52			47.52	0.00
16														
17		TOTALS				367.05	628.73	710.77	27.44	601.29	0.00	0.00	628.73	27.44
18		AVERAGE				36.71	62.87	71.08	2.74	60.13	ERROR	ERROR	62.87	2.74
19		MAXIMUM				42.20	84.82	125.77	9.41	75.41	0.00	0.00	84.82	9.41
20		MINIMUM				28.00	47.52	37.12	0.00	47.52	0.00	0.00	47.52	0.00
21														
22														
23														
24	JOB GP	RATE/HR												
25														
26	1	1.50												
27	2	1.60												
28	3	1.95												
29	4	2.01												
30	5	2.43												
31														

The ERRORs are caused by trying to calculate the average of a range of empty cells.

Now we need to save columns M and N in DIF format as follows. Place the cursor on cell M6 (the top left-hand corner of the data block to be saved), type /S#S and give the file to be saved a name. The # indicates the file is to be saved in DIF format. Now type N20 (i.e. the bottom right-hand corner of the data to be saved). In the next prompt, ("Data Save: R C or RETURN"), "R" means "save the block row by row", "C" means "save it column by column". If it doesn't matter which way, (as in this case) just press "return". Now save the whole sheet in the normal way (ie /SS). To recall the year-to-date figures just saved as the old year-to-date figures, place the cursor in cell K6, type /S#L, give the DIF file name and press return. Two identical sets of year-to-date figures will appear in columns K to N. Now press "!". The figures in columns G and I will be added to those now in columns K and L to give the new year-to-date totals in columns M and N. Columns K to N should now look like fig.28 (Provided the column width is increased to eight characters.)

Fig.28

K	L	M	N
OLD YEAR-T-D		NEW YEAR T-D	
GROSS PAY	TAX PAID	GROSS PAY	TAX PAID
55.80	5.61	111.60	11.21
64.00	5.35	128.00	10.71
71.18	0.00	142.35	0.00
84.82	9.41	169.64	18.81
72.74	1.92	145.47	3.83
54.60	0.00	109.20	0.00
61.60	5.15	123.20	10.31
59.10	0.00	118.20	0.00
57.38	0.00	114.75	0.00
47.52	0.00	95.04	0.00
628.73	27.44	1257.45	54.87
62.87	2.74	125.75	5.49
84.82	9.41	169.64	18.82
47.52	0.00	95.04	0.00

Save this as PAY28.

Now change a few of the hours worked figures to simulate correction of errors and recalculate the sheet. The new year-to-date figures will be corrected. Try pressing "!" again. The figures do not change. So you can see that using DIF files allows you to accumulate totals accurately and easily. The advantage of this is that, for example, a master worksheet, fully formatted but as yet without any data in it can be stored for use in successive months. The previous month's year-to-date totals would be recalled from a DIF file, the current month's data added and the new year-to-date figures stored as a DIF file, ready for next month. Meanwhile, the current month's worksheet is stored under another name so that the master ("template") is not damaged. Chapter 17 covers the creation and use of templates.

It is possible to save a block of data column by column and to recall it row by row. To try this, place the cursor on cell K6, type /S#S, give the DIF file a name and then type N20. When the prompt

```
Data Save: R C or RETURN
```

appears, press C to save the data column by column. Now place the cursor on cell D23 (say) and type /S#L. Type the DIF file name and answer R to the "R C or RETURN" prompt. The data will be recalled but what was saved as column K will now appear as row 23. Column L will be recalled as row 24 and so on. Rows 23 to 26 from column D onwards will now look like fig.29.

Fig.29

55.8	64	71.175	84.822	72.735	54.6	61.6	59.1	57.375	47.52	-628.727	62.8727	84.822	47.52
5.60538	5.35385	0	9.40814	1.91665	0	5.15308	0	0	0	-27.4371	2.74371	9.40814	0
111.6	128	142.35	169.644	145.47	109.2	123.2	118.2	114.75	95.04	-1257.45	125.745	169.644	95.04
11.2108	10.7077	0	18.8163	3.83331	0	10.3062	0	0	0	-54.8742	5.48742	18.8163	0

Since these cells were not pre-formatted, the data is displayed to the greatest precision required and allowed by the column width.

RECAP

DIF (Data Interchange Format) files can pass data to and from VisiCalc worksheets and other programs such as plotting programs. Parts of a worksheet can be saved either row by row or column by column and recalled the same way, or they can be saved row by row and recalled column by column and vice versa.

/S#S saves part (or all) of the worksheet in DIF format. The cursor is placed in the top left hand corner of the block of cells to be saved, /S#S is typed, the file name is specified, the lower right-hand corner cell co-ordinates are given and row-by-row (R), column-by-column (C) or "don't care" (return) is specified. "Don't care" is actually the same as "R" for rows.

/S#L loads a DIF file back into a worksheet. The cursor is placed in the top left-hand corner of the target part of the worksheet, /S#L is typed, the DIF file name given and row-by-row (R), column-by-column (C) or "don't care" (return) specified. A file saved row-by-row may be recalled column-by-column, and vice versa.

13

Datagrams or command files

These are not officially part of VisiCalc so you won't find any information in your VisiCalc manual, but they work very effectively on the Apple II. However, they may not work properly on other computers, especially those based on the 8080 or Z80 microprocessors. The only way to find out whether they work on your computer is to try them and see!

In essence, datagrams are keyboard commands stored on disk. They consist of the "goto" (〉) command followed by the cell co-ordinates to which the command is to be applied. These are separated from the command itself by a colon (:). The command can be almost anything, but typically it might look like "#+F6" which means "add the value in F6 to the value already in the cell". Commands are typed as labels in any convenient part of any worksheet (not necessarily the worksheet to which the commands will be applied). It is vital that the whole command be visible on the screen so the column width must be set appropriately wide. The commands are saved on disk using /PF (i.e. print to a file) and the file name must end in ".VC" if your computer uses the CP/M operating system. The command file is applied to the worksheet by using /SL followed by the command file name.

Datagrams are an alternative method of producing cumulative figures. A worksheet can be completed and checked, and then a datagram loaded to calculate cumulative totals. The following example (fig.30) illustrates their use:

```
Fig.30    A       B        C        D        E        F         G        H        I        J        K         L         M
  1                        .                                  TAX RATE % 30                    YEAR-TO-DATE
  2-----------------------------------------------------------------------------------------------------------
  3    EMP.     EMP.     JOB      TAX   HOURLY   HOURS     GROSS     FREE      TAX      NET   GROSS      TAX
  4   NUMB.     NAME   GROUP     CODE     RATE  WORKED       PAY      PAY      DUE      PAY   PAY       PAID
  5-----------------------------------------------------------------------------------------------------------
  6    0052    BROWN       1      193     1.50   37.20     55.80    37.12     5.61    50.19                    )K6:#+G6
  7    0098    GREEN       2      240     1.60   40.00     64.00    46.15     5.35    58.65                    )K7:#+G7
  8    0133    BLACK       3      432     1.95   36.50     71.18    83.08     0.00    71.18                    )K8:#+G8
  9    1432    WHITE       4      278     2.01   42.20     84.82    53.46     9.41    75.41                    )K9:#+G9
 10    1545    JONES       3      345     1.95   37.30     72.74    66.35     1.92    70.82                    )K10:#+G10
 11    2386    VANCE       3      654     1.95   28.00     54.60   125.77     0.00    54.60                    )K11:#+G11
 12    2912    EVANS       2      231     1.60   38.50     61.60    44.42     5.15    56.45                    )K12:#+G12
 13    3005     KING       1      510     1.50   39.40     59.10    98.08     0.00    59.10                    )K13:#+G13
 14    3112    BAKER       1      488     1.50   38.25     57.38    93.85     0.00    57.38                    )K14:#+G15
 15    3610    SMITH       2      325     1.60   29.70     47.52    62.50     0.00    47.52                    )K15:#+G16
 16-----------------------------------------------------------------------------------------------------------)L6:#+I6
 17             TOTALS                             367.05    628.73   710.77    27.44   601.29    0.00      0.00)L7:#+I7
 18            AVERAGE                              36.71     62.87    71.08     2.74    60.13   ERROR     ERROR)L8:#+I8
 19            MAXIMUM                              42.20     84.82   125.77     9.41    75.41    0.00      0.00)L9:#+I9
 20            MINIMUM                              28.00     47.52    37.12     0.00    47.52    0.00      0.00)L10:#+I10
 21===========================================================================================================)L11:#+I11
 22                                                                                                            )L12:#+I12
 23                                                                                                            )L13:#+I13
 24  JOB GP RATE/HR                                                                                            )L14:#+I14
 25---------------
 26       1    1.50
 27       2    1.60
 28       3    1.95
 29       4    2.01
 30       5    2.43
 31
```

The apparently empty year-to-date columns are actually pre-formatted using /F$. The datagram occupies cells M6 to M25. Each cell must contain a label, so press the quotes (") key as the first character typed into each cell. Since the complete contents of each cell must appear on the screen, increase the column width to ten characters until the datagram has been stored. Then return the column width to eight characters. The first cell in the datagram means "send the cursor to K6 (⟩K6), fix the value already there (#), and place into cell K6 the formula that will add the value in G6 to this existing value (+G6)", i.e. accumulate the value in G6 into K6. For example, if G6 already contains the value 55.8 and K6 is blank (or contains the value zero), the formula placed in K6 by the datagram will be "0 + G6", giving the value 55.8. If the value in G6 is changed and the sheet re-calculated, the values in columns K and L will change. To store the datagram on disk, place the cursor on the first entry, type /PF, give the file name (ending with .VC if your computer uses the CP/M operating system) and specify the co-ordinates of the last datagram cell. Now return the column width to eight. This stored version cannot be inspected using VisiCalc, so make sure you store another version using /SS. It could, however, be inspected using a word processing programme such as Applewriter II or Wordstar, or by means of a program written in BASIC. To use the datagram, load the worksheet to which the datagram is to be applied, make any changes (such as hours worked this week, etc.) and re-calculate the sheet. Check the results are acceptable. Now apply the datagram by typing /SL and the datagram name. (It is not necessary to add .VC to the datagram name – under

CP/M /SL assumes the file name ends in .VC anyway). The commands contained in the datagram will be applied to the worksheet. Since the above example contains calculations which depend on data produced by applying the datagram, the sheet may need to be recalculated to complete the job. Corrections can be made to the sheet and the cumulative figures in columns K and L will be recalculated correctly. The results should look something like fig.31.

Try changing the hours worked (as if for the next week), recalculating the sheet and then re-applying the datagram. The results should be true year-to-date figures. Recalculating the sheet again will not affect these year-to-date figures. Applying the datagram again will add the current gross pay and tax due into the cumulative figures to produce new year-to-dates.

However, if "#" is added at the end of each cell in the datagram, then the command in cell M6 means "send the cursor to cell K6 (⟩K6), fix the current value in K6(#), add the value in G6 to that already in K6 (+G6) and fix the result (#)". Further recalculation cannot change the year-to-date figures, even if G6 is changed and then the sheet recalculated. Re-application of this datagram also results in the gross pay and tax due figures being added to the year-to-dates.

```
Fig.31   A      B       C      D      E      F       G      H       I      J      K       L
   1                                                 TAX  RATE % 30
   2-------------------------------------------------------------------------YEAR-TO-DATE
   3   EMP.   EMP.     JOB    TAX HOURLY  HOURS   GROSS    FREE    TAX    NET  GROSS     TAX
   4  NUMB.   NAME   GROUP   CODE  RATE  WORKED     PAY     PAY    DUE    PAY  PAY      PAID
   5-------------------------------------------------------------------------------------
   6   0052  BROWN       1    193   1.50  37.20   55.80   37.12   5.61  50.19  55.80   5.61
   7   0098  GREEN       2    240   1.60  40.00   64.00   46.15   5.35  58.65  64.00   5.35
   8   0133  BLACK       3    432   1.95  36.50   71.18   83.08   0.00  71.18  71.18   0.00
   9   1432  WHITE       4    278   2.01  42.20   84.82   53.46   9.41  75.41  84.82   9.41
  10   1545  JONES       3    345   1.95  37.30   72.74   66.35   1.92  70.82  72.74   1.92
  11   2386  VANCE       3    654   1.95  28.00   54.60  125.77   0.00  54.60  54.60   0.00
  12   2912  EVANS       2    231   1.60  38.50   61.60   44.42   5.15  56.45  61.60   5.15
  13   3005   KING       1    510   1.50  39.40   59.10   98.08   0.00  59.10  59.10   0.00
  14   3112  BAKER       1    488   1.50  38.25   57.38   93.85   0.00  57.38  57.38   0.00
  15   3610  SMITH       2    325   1.60  29.70   47.52   62.50   0.00  47.52  47.52   0.00
  16-------------------------------------------------------------------------------------
  17          TOTALS                        367.05  628.73  710.77  27.44 601.29 628.73  27.44
  18         AVERAGE                         36.71   62.87   71.08   2.74  60.13  62.87   2.74
  19         MAXIMUM                         42.20   84.82  125.77   9.41  75.41  84.82   9.41
  20         MINIMUM                         28.00   47.52   37.12   0.00  47.52  47.52   0.00
  21=====================================================================================
  22
  23
  24 JOB GP RATE/HR
  25 --------------
  26       1   1.50
  27       2   1.60
  28       3   1.95
  29       4   2.01
  30       5   2.43
  31
```

RECAP

DATAGRAMS or command files consist of a series of "goto" commands followed by calculation instructions. They are typed into a worksheet as labels and stored on disk for later use by using /PF. The file name must have .VC added to its end if a CP/M based computer is being used. Since the contents of datagram files cannot be inspected, a separate copy must be stored using the normal /SS command. The datagram is applied to the displayed worksheet merely by loading it using /SL.

For example, "⟩K6:#+G6" means "place the cursor on cell K6. Into this cell place the formula which will add the number currently in cell G6 to whatever number is in K6." If K6 contains the value 65.4 then the formula which will be placed in K6 is "65.4 + G6". This allows changes in the value in G6 to be reflected in column K when the sheet is re-calculated.

If the value in K6 is 23.6, then "⟩K6:#+G6#" (i.e. the above datagram with # added to the end) produces the formula "65.4 + 23.6" which does not allow any changes in G6 to be reflected in column K when the sheet is re-calculated.

NOTE Datagrams are not an official part of VisiCalc and they do not appear in the VisiCalc manual. Experience has shown they work reliably on the Apple II, but they are not reliable on some other computers. It is worth experimenting with them on your computer, though, since they are so useful.

14

Discounted cash flow and net present value

A pound in the hand is worth two in the sweet by and by. Or is it? It's certainly true that a pound now is worth more than a pound in a year's time, even if inflation is ignored. A pound invested now will be worth more than a pound in a year's time, so a promise of a pound at the end of the year must be worth somewhat less than a pound payable today. To take an extreme example, if a pound invested today could earn 10 % compound interest, then the promise of a pound in 50 years time is the equivalent of offerring 8.5p right now! And that's before inflation is allowed for. Investment appraisal is a complex subject – much too complex to be discussed in detail here. However a simple example will illustrate the use of the VisiCalc function @NPV ("net present value").

Suppose that a sum of money is invested today and the annual returns on that investment are estimated over a period of five years. What rate of interest is it earning? Is a second project more worth while? To answer these questions involves calculations which, by hand, involve the use of discounted cash flow tables that are generally expressed to at least four places of decimals. Using VisiCalc, @NPV takes care of all the tables and makes the arithmetic very simple.

Take the following example, for instance:

	A	B	C	D	E	F
1	PROJECT A			PROJECT B		
2	---------			---------		
3	INTEREST RATE %		10	INTEREST RATE %		10
4	INVESTED	20000		INVESTED	20000	
5						
6	RETURN			RETURN		
7	IN YEAR			IN YEAR		
8	1	3000		1	15000	
9	2	7500		2	25000	
10	3	15000		3	21500	
11	4	25000		4	14500	
12	5	30000		5	4500	
13						
14	TOTAL	80500		TOTAL	80500	
15						
16	PRESENT	55898		PRESENT	63149	
17	VALUE			VALUE		
18						
19	PRESENT	35898		PRESENT	43149	
20	NET VALUE			NET VALUE		
21						
22						

The formula used in cell C16 to calculate the present value of the investment is

```
@NPV(C3/100,B8...B12)
```

which, translated, means "calculate the net present value of the cash flows at the end of years 1 to 5 in cells B8 to B12 using the rate of interest in cell C3 expressed as a fraction". Experimenting with the interest rates for each of the two projects to bring the present net value to zero shows that the second project earns a higher percentage rate of return since the cash returns are higher in the earlier years. (Try using rates of approximately 46 % for project A and 86 % for project B.)

15

Hints and tips

1. Put the co-ordinates of the top left and bottom right-hand cells for printout in cell A1, the file name in cell A2, the version date in A3, a description of the spreadsheet in cell A4 and the co-ordinates of the bottom right hand corner in cell A5. Pad each entry with enough blanks on the left to hide each entry in normal use and then either widen the columns (temporarily) in order to make the entries visible, or merely place the cursor on the appropriate cell and read its contents at the top of the screen.
2. To speed data entry, switch off automatic calculation using /GCM. Inititiate recalculation by pressing the ! key.
3. The destination cell of a 'goto' (⟩) can be positioned at the top left of the screen by using /X before the ⟩. This is not an official VisiCalc command but it seems to work reliably.
4. If a printout will not be of the whole sheet, then place the co-ordinates of the top left and bottom right-hand corners in a cell or cells just outside the area to be printed as a reminder.
5. Normally the formulae and other cell contents can only be printed out by means of a word processing program or by using a program written in BASIC. However, on the Apple, using /SS,S1 instead of /P results in the cell formulae etc. being sent to the printer (in slot 1) instead of to the floppy disk. If your printer is not in slot 1, then substitute the actual slot number for the '1'. A word processing programme can be used in the conventional way to examine a VisiCalc file by displaying all the cell contents, one cell to a line. An unconventional way is to globally change all the colons (:) to colons followed by quotes (:")and save the result. As a result, the contents of every cell have been converted into label format. This is then loaded backinto VisiCalc as if it were an ordinary VisiCalc worksheet – which, of course, it is. Since every cell now contains a label, the formulae can be displayed on the screen (and therefore printed), provided the column width is sufficiently great. Of course, no calculation can be performed on such a modified worksheet!
6. On the Apple II, a quick two finger tattoo on the Q and ESC keys will start 'label' mode in a cell more quickly than typing ". It's not so convenient on the Apple IIe, though. This may be true of other computers as well, depending on their keyboard layouts.
7. To enter a value which is the result of an 'off screen' calculation, don't reach for your hand calculator to work out the value. Instead, type the formula into a cell, type # to evaluate the expression, then type 'return' or press an arrow key. The formula may include the cell co-ordinates of a cell which already contains either a value or another formula (see chapter 11).
8. When entering a complex formula involving references to other cells, move the cursor to the cell referred to and carry on typing whatever comes immediately after the cell reference. VisiCalc automatically will pick up the co-ordinates of that cell and incorporate them into the formula.
9. To round a positive number 'N' to 'D' decimal places, use the formula

   ```
   @INT(N * 10 * D + .5) / 10 * D
   ```

   For negative numbers, substitute a minus for the plus. This does not add padding zeroes to the end of numbers having fewer than the requested number of decimal places but this could be done, if desperately required, using a word processing package. /F$ rounds to two decimal places and adds zeroes as necessary, however.
10. The built in functions such as @SUM(can be abbreviated to @S(. VisiCalc automatically will supply the missing characters. Other functions can be abbreviated in a similar fashion. @MAX and @MIN are abbreviated to @MA and @MI, however.
11. @COUNT treats a zero as if it were a blank (i.e. ignores it) in some versions of VisiCalc.

12. On computers with four arrow keys, when in edit mode (/E) the up arrow moves the cursor to the first character and the down arrow to the last character in the string being edited.

13. The four cursor key movements can be duplicated using CTRL-K for up, CTRL-J for down, CTRL-H for left and CTRL-U for right on some computers. (Also, Return = CTRL-M.)

14. Starting and finishing ranges on cells containing labels allows rows or columns to be inserted anywhere within the range of cells.

15. The same information can be formatted in two different ways and both ways displayed on the screen by splitting the screen using /W. Thus each window can have its own column width, etc.

16. If you've forgotten a file name, or have files with long names liable to be mistyped, type /SL and press the right arrow key. The first VisiCalc file name on the disk will be displayed. If this is the file you want to load, press "return". If not, keep pressing the right arrow until the correct file name appears. If you accidentally pass the required file name, CTRL-C will cancel the command and allow you to start all over again. If the file is on drive 2, type /SL,D2 for the Apple or /SLB: for CP/M. Similarly, if the name under which a file is to be saved has been forgotten (or is too long and complicated to get right first time), then type /SS and press the right arrow until the correct file name is displayed. Then press "return". If you wish to alter a file name that is displayed on the edit line, press ESC. You may now edit the displayed file name. This can be useful if you use meaningful but long file names on the Apple and you merely wish to change a version number in the filename, for example.

17. Memory released by shrinking the size of the worksheet is not recovered by VisiCalc until the sheet is saved and re-loaded.

18. DIF files do not contain formulae, only labels and values. They do not contain anything (such as a dotted line) produced by /-. Only the /- and the repetition character appear. This is not translated back into a dotted line when the DIF file is re-loaded.

19. VisiCalc can be used as a primitive word processor by using a column width almost equal to the screen width. This means that one line of text occupies one cell and so can be edited using /E. Extra lines can be inserted using /IR, lines deleted using /DR, and lines moved using /MR.

20. Think before keying! A lot of wasted effort can then be avoided.

21. Debug by inserting easily checked data and then pressing the ! key.

22. Keep an eye on the memory indicator. If there's too little memory left for data, then reduce the length and number of labels. Labels are memory hungry and can often be abbreviated.

23. Make backup copies of your data disks! If you have two drives, save the file twice – once on each drive. Recall the file name using tip 16, save the file on drive 1 then recall the file name again. Add ",D2" to the name and save again.

16

Clangers – what NOT to do!

The following are some of the commoner clangers dropped by both beginners and experts:

1. Omitting to make backup copies of files, either through forgetfulness or over-confidence. Disks do go wrong and the law of universal cussedness states that you will almost have finished that rush job that took half a day just when the disk fails and you lose the lot!
2. Saving multiple versions of a file using variously mistyped versions of the file name. Which is the latest version? See hints and tips numbers 16 and 23 for ways of avoiding this clanger.
3. Circular references in formulae can never produce a correct result. Forward references do not produce the correct results except when recalculation is performed twice.
4. Overlaying one sheet on another without first clearing the screen. It's easy to amalgamate two or more sheets, but it's impossible to disentangle the result! Overlaying one sheet on another may be done deliberately, however – see chapter 17.
5. Getting rows and columns the wrong way round. Once you've decided what should be columns and what should be rows and have created the spreadsheet, it's too late to change your mind and exchange rows for columns – it can't be done! So think before keying.
6. Over-writing cells containing formulae. Typing data into formulae cells destroys the formulae – and wrecks the sheet. Chapter 17 suggests ways of minimising this danger.

17

Template design

A template is a spreadsheet containing all the permanent labels, values and formulae necessary to produce a finished result. It only requires the addition of current data to produce the report.

The uses of a spreadsheet are limited only by the imagination of the user but the actual size of the sheet available to the user is limited by the amount of memory available in your computer in which to hold the information 'written' onto the sheet. Herein lies a trap for the unwary beginner. If you try typing anything in the bottom right-hand cell (BK254) you will see that VisiCalc will not accept the entry (unless you are extremely fortunate and have a very large amount of memory available). VisiCalc requires about 29k bytes of memory. The rest is available for the actual spreadsheet. VisiCalc looks after this automatically. Moving the cursor to a cell does not affect the actual size of the worksheet until something is written into that cell. Each empty cell requires two bytes of memory and labels require one byte per character. Only enough memory to hold the contents of a cell is used, so that memory is not wasted by allocating more memory than is necessary. This is called "dynamic memory allocation".

We now know that we can't use the entire sheet. So, how much can we use? Basically, the more columns the less rows, and vice versa. Do keep an eye on the free memory indicator in the top right hand corner of the screen. If you have finished a template and the memory indicator is very low, there may not be enough memory left to allow all the data to be entered. Labels occupy more space than values (one byte per label character) so avoid unnecessary text if memory is at a premium.

Every time a template under construction is extended either to the right or downwards, VisiCalc re-builds its internal index and this can cause a perceptible delay. To overcome this problem make an educated guess as to where the final bottom right hand cell will be – push it out a bit further and type anything into it. At this point if the memory indicator is low it is unlikely that there will be enough available memory left in which to store all the labels, values and formulae. This saves you the heartache of nearly completing an elaborate template and finding you have run out of memory. Once the template is complete, blank out the original bottom right hand cell, save the file, reload it and examine the memory indicator, and you will find that the unused memory has been recovered. This is also a useful trick if you find that memory is running critically low and there are fewer columns or rows than originally estimated.

A lot of these problems can be minimised by sketching out your ideas on paper before laying a finger on the keyboard. This becomes even more vital when designing templates with interlocking sections (for example, cashflow forecast in chapter 18), because if you have finished the first section and are working on an adjacent section and need to insert or delete a row or column, you may find that you have destroyed part of the first section as well!

For example, deleting row 4 in section 2 will also delete row 4 in section 1.

```
        Section 1                     Section 2
-----------------------------------------------------
!   A   B   C   D   E   !     !   M   N   O   P   !
!1                      !     !                   !
!2                      !     !                   !
!3                      !     !                   !
!4                      !     !                   !
!5                      !     !                   !
!6                      !     !                   !
!7                      !     !                   !
-----------------------------------------------------
```

The solution is to design each section independently and 'overlay' them one on the other to form the completed template. Having designed section 1, save it and clear the screen. Create section 2 in the exact position it will occupy in the completed template (ie columns M to P and rows 1 to 7 in the above example). Having saved it DO NOT CLEAR THE SCREEN. Now load section 1 back into memory, complete the formulae linking the sections and there is the completed template. This method can be used to link as many sections as you require. Don't forget to save each section individually as it is not as easy to split a template into its individual sections as it is to combine them.

Having completed the template, save it before entering any data. This then becomes the master which can be recalled at any time and a fresh set of data entered.

Points to remember...

1. Don't try and build too complex a model straight away. Remember the old adage – learn to walk before you run.
2. Even when you are expert still try to keep your templates as simple as possible – try not to be complex for complexity's sake.
3. If you are designing a template for others to use, make it easy for them to see where to enter data. Remember, they didn't create it so they don't know their way around it as you do – if necessary provide written instructions. Another way is to have a data entry area and a separate report area. This keeps your formulae away from accidental over-typing (for example, VAT book in chapter 18). Finally it is also possible to 'lock' the formulae behind titles fixed by using /T.
4. Set global column widths to allow for the largest value you envisage using. Nothing is more frustrating than typing text which overflows to the next column, then finding that you have to widen the column width to accommodate large figures and having to retype all the text.

Finally, do a number of test runs before using the template seriously – you may have quite a bit of de-bugging to do! Use simple numbers that you can check manually without too much brain strain!

18

Financial templates

1 Invoicing

Typing the name and address of each customer for each invoice is a tedious process, particularly if it is a regular customer. Each customer name and address can be stored in a separate DIF file and loaded into the appropriate invoice as required. The rest of the invoice copes automatically with VAT and discounts.

2 VAT book

The dreaded Customs and Excise insist on a VAT book being kept as well as your cash book – so here it is!

3 Cashflow forecasting

A cashflow forecast enables you to see how much money actually is received and spent in any given month, which enables you to plan future expenditure.

Page 1 (employment costs)
Fill in names and basic salaries as appropriate and indicate extra staff numbers only in the month in which you wish to employ them.

Page 2 (sales forecast)
When planning cashflow we are only concerned with when you receive payment rather than when the work is completed. We assume here that payment will be made two months after invoicing but this can be adjusted easily if you so require.

Page 3 (cashflow forecast)
For cashflow purpose, fill in the outgoings in the month payment is made, NOT in the month the bill is received. Employment and sales are carried forward to the cashflow forecast automatically.

4 Extended trial balance and profit and loss account

The basic difference between cashflow and profit and loss (P & L) is that cashflow records the income and outgoings in the month in which payment is made and P & L records the incoming and outgoings in the month in which goods and services are supplied.

This template is designed for those companies who maintain a nominal (general) ledger.

	A	B	C	D	E
1		JOE BLOGGS & SON			
2					
3					
4		INVOICE NO			0
5					
6	CUSTOMER				
7	ADDRESS				
8	ADDRESS				
9	ADDRESS				
10	POST CODE				
11					
12					
13				ITEM	
14	ITEM		QUANTITY	COST	TOTAL
15					
16			....	....	0
17			....	....	0
18			....	....	0
19			....	....	0
20			....	....	0
21			....	....	0
22			....	....	0
23			....	....	0
24					
25		SUB TOTAL		0	0
26					
27					
28					
29	DISCOUNT @ (%) 0				0
30					
31					
32	PLUS VAT @ (%) 15				0
33					
34					
35	TOTAL PAYABLE				0
36					
37					
38					
39					
40					
41					
42					
43					
44					
45					
46		AMOUNT	% DISCOUNT		
47					
48		0	0		
49		500	2		
50		1000	3		
51		1500	4		
52		2000	5		
53		2500	6		
54		3000	7		
55		3500	8		
56		4000	9		
57		4500	10		
58		5000	12		

TEMPLATE FOR INVOICING

```
>B58:12
>A58:5000
>B57:10
>A57:4500
>B56:9
>A56:4000
>B55:8
>A55:3500
>B54:7
>A54:3000
>B53:6
>A53:2500
>B52:5
>A52:2000
>B51:4
>A51:1500
>B50:3
>A50:1000
>B49:2
>A49:500
>B48:0
>A48:0
>C47:"——
>B47:/—
>A47:/—
>C46:"SCOUNT
>B46:/FR" % DI
>A46:/FR"AMOUNT
>D45:/—
>C45:/—
>B45:/—
>A45:/—
>E36:/-=
>E35:@SUM(D25-E29+E32)
>D35:"BLE
>C35:/FR"OTAL PAYA
>B35:/FR"T
>E34:/-=
>E32:@SUM((D25-E29*D32)/100)
>D32:/FL15
>C32:/FR"VAT @ (%)
>B32:/FR"PLUS
>A32:/FR
>C31:/FR
>B31:/FR
>E29:+D25*(D29/100)
>D29:/FL@LOOKUP(D25,A48...A58)
>C29:/FR"UNT @ (%)
>B29:/FR"DISCO
>A29:/FR
>D28:/FL
>C28:/FR
>B28:/FL
>D26:/—
>A26:/FR
>E25:+D25
>D25:@SUM(D16...D23)
>C25:"B TOTAL
>B25:/FR"SU
>E24:/—
>D24:/—
>C24:/—
>B24:/—
>A24:/—
>D23:+B23*C23
>C23:/FR"....
>B23:/FR"....
>D22:+B22*C22
>C22:/FR"....
>B22:/FR"....
>A22:/FL
>D21:+B21*C21
>C21:/FR"....
>B21:/FR"....
>A21:/FL
>D20:+B20*C20
>C20:/FR"....
>B20:/FR"....
>D19:+B19*C19
>C19:/FR"....
>B19:/FR"....
>D18:+B18*C18
>C18:/FR"....
>B18:/FR"....
>D17:+B17*C17
>C17:/FR"....
>B17:/FR"....
>D16:+B16*C16
>C16:/FR"....
>B16:/FR"....
>D15:/—
>C15:/—
>B15:/—
>A15:/—
>D14:/FR"TOTAL
>C14:/FR"COST
>B14:/FR"QUANTITY
>A14:/FL"ITEM
>C13:/FR"ITEM
>D12:/—
>C12:/—
>B12:/—
>A12:/—
>A10:"POST CODE
>A9:"ADDRESS
>A8:"ADDRESS
>A7:"ADDRESS
>A6:"CUSTOMER
>D4:/FIO
>C4:"INVOICE NO
>B4:/FR"I
>C2:/-=
>B2:/-=
>C1:"GS & SON
>B1:" JOE BLOGG
/W1
/GOC
/GRA
/GFI
/GC9
/X!/X>A1:>A1:
```

```
         A      B      C      D      E      F      G      H      I      J      K      L      M      N
   ------------------------------------------------------------------------------------------------
 1  VAT BOOK—QUARTERLY         JOE BLOGGS AND SON
 2  ==================         ==================

 3  MONTH 1
 4  -------                               V.A.T. BOOK
 5  TOTAL BANKED.....  ....               -----------
 6
 7  TOTAL VAT (OUTPUT) ....               RECEIPTS                        PAYMENTS
 8                                        --------                        --------
 9  TOTAL CHEQUES....  ....    PERIOD                (BOX 1)  (BOX 9)                 (BOX 5)  (BOX 10)    (BOX 8)
10                                        GROSS               VALUE OF    GROSS                 VALUE OF        NET
11  TOTAL VAT (INPUT). ....               TOTAL         VAT   OUTPUTS     TOTAL           VAT    INPUTS     PAYABLE
12                             ------------------------------------------------------------------------------------
13  -----------------------
14  MONTH 2
15  -------                    MONTH       0.00        0.00      0.00      0.00          0.00      0.00
16  TOTAL BANKED.....  ....    MONTH       0.00        0.00      0.00      0.00          0.00      0.00
17                             MONTH       0.00        0.00      0.00      0.00          0.00      0.00
18  TOTAL VAT (OUTPUT) ....               ---------------------------------------------------------------------
19                             TOTALS      0.00        0.00      0.00      0.00          0.00      0.00       0.00
20  TOTAL CHEQUES....  ....               =====================================================================
21
22  TOTAL VAT (INPUT). ....
23
24  -------------------------------
25  MONTH 3
26  -------
27  TOTAL BANKED...... ....
28
29  TOTAL VAT (OUTPUT) ....
30
31  TOTAL CHEQUES..... ....
32
33  TOTAL VAT (INPUT). ....
```

```
>C33:/FR"....
>B33:" (INPUT).
>A33:"TOTAL VAT
>C31:/FR"....
>B31:"QUES.....
>A31:"TOTAL CHE
>C29:/FR"....
>B29:" (OUTPUT)
>A29:"TOTAL VAT
>C27:/FR"....
>B27:"KED......
>A27:"TOTAL BANKE
>A26:"———
>A25:"MONTH 3
>C24:/—
>B24:/—
>A24:/—
>C22:/FR"....
>B22:" (INPUT).
>A22:"TOTAL VAT
>N20:/-=
>M20:/-=
```

```
>L20:/-=
>K20:/-=
>J20:/-=
>I20:/-=
>H20:/-=
>G20:/-=
>F20:/-=
>C20:/FR"....
>B20:"QUES.....
>A20:"TOTAL CHE
>N19:@SUM(G19-K19)
>L19:@SUM(L15...L17)
>K19:@SUM(K15...K17)
>J19:@SUM(J15...J17)
>H19:@SUM(H15...H17)
>G19:@SUM(G15...G17)
>F19:@SUM(F15...F17)
>E19:"TOTALS
>N18:/—
>M18:/—
>L18:/—
>K18:/—
```

```
>J18:/-
>I18:/-
>H18:/-
>G18:/-
>F18:/-
>C18:/FR"....
>B18:" (OUTPUT)
>A18:"TOTAL VAT
>L17:@SUM(J17-K17)
>K17:+C33
>J17:+C31
>H17:@SUM(F17-G17)
>G17:+C29
>F17:+C27
>E17:"MONTH
>L16:@SUM(J16-K16)
>K16:+C22
>J16:+C20
>H16:@SUM(F16-G16)
>G16:+C18
>F16:+C16
>E16:"MONTH
>C16:/FR"....
>B16:"KED......
>A16:"TOTAL BANKE
>L15:@SUM(J15-K15)
>K15:+C11
>J15:+C9
>H15:@SUM(F15-G15)
>G15:+C7
>F15:+C5
>E15:"MONTH
>A15:"———
>A14:"MONTH 2
>C13:/-
>B13:/-
>A13:/-
>N12:/-
>M12:/-
>L12:/-
>K12:/-
>J12:/-
>I12:/-
>H12:/-
>G12:/-
>F12:/-
>E12:/-
>N11:" PAYABLE
>L11:"  INPUTS
>K11:"    VAT
>J11:"   TOTAL
>H11:" OUTPUTS
>G11:"    VAT
>F11:"   TOTAL
>C11:/FR"....
>B11:" (INPUT).
>A11:"TOTAL VAT
>N10:"    NET
>L10:" VALUE OF
>J10:"   GROSS
>H10:" VALUE OF
>F10:"   GROSS
>N9:"  (BOX 8)
>L9:"  (BOX 10)
>K9:"  (BOX 5)
>H9:"  (BOX 9)
>G9:"  (BOX 1)
>E9:"PERIOD
>C9:/FR"....
>B9:"QUES.....
>A9:"TOTAL CHE
>J8:"———
>F8:"———
>J7:"PAYMENTS
>F7:"RECEIPTS
>C7:/FR"....
>B7:" (OUTPUT)
>A7:"TOTAL VAT
>H5:"——
>G5:"  ——
>C5:/FR"....
>B5:"KED......
>A5:"TOTAL BANKE
>H4:"BOOK
>G4:"  V.A.T.
>A4:"———
>A3:"MONTH 1
>F2:/-=
>E2:/-=
>C2:"==
>B2:/-=
>A2:/-=
>F1:"S AND SON
>E1:"JOE BLOGG
>C1:"LY
>B1:"- QUARTER
>A1:"VAT BOOK
/W1
/GOC
/GRA
/GF$
/GC9
/X-/X>A1:>A1:
```

	A B	C	D	E	F	G	H	I	
1	PAGE 1			EMPLOYMENT COSTS					
2									
3	FINANCIAL YEAR		****.*						
4	PREPARED	DD.M	JAN.	FEB.	MARCH	APRIL	MAY	JUNE	TOTAL
5									
6		BASIC							
7		SALARY							
8	DIRECTORS								
9	NAME	....	0	0	0	0	0	0	0
10	NAME	....	0	0	0	0	0	0	0
11									
12	SALES STAFF								
13	NAME	....	0	0	0	0	0	0	0
14	NAME	....	0	0	0	0	0	0	0
15	NAME	....	0	0	0	0	0	0	0
16	NAME	....	0	0	0	0	0	0	0
17	NAME	....	0	0	0	0	0	0	0
18									
19	EXTRA STAFF NO'S		0	0	0	0	0	0	
20		ERROR							
21	SENIOR £	0	0	0	0	0	0	0	0
22									
23	TOTAL PROFESSIONAL								
24	STAFF		0	0	0	0	0	0	
25									
26	ADMINISTRATION STAFF								
27									
28	NAME	....	0	0	0	0	0	0	0
29	NAME	....	0	0	0	0	0	0	0
30	NAME		0	0	0	0	0	0	0
31		PER PERS							
32	TYPIST NO'S			0	0	0	0	0	0
33	TYPIST £	250	0	0	0	0	0	0	0
34									
35	TOTAL SALARIES		0	0	0	0	0	0	
36									
37	NIC AVE	.13							
38	EMPLOYERS N.I.C.		0	0	0	0	0	0	0
39									
40	GRAND TOTAL		0	0	0	0	0	0	0
41									
42	TOTAL STAFF NO'S		0	0	0	0	0	0	
43									
44									
45	CASH FLOW EXTRACT								
46									
47	ASSUMPTION — PAYE AND NIC WILL BE								
48		1/3 OF TOTAL EMPLOYMENT COSTS							
49									
50	NET EMPLOYMENT								
51		COSTS	0	0	0	0	0	0	0
52	PAYE & NIC		....	0	0	0	0	0	0
53									
54		TOTAL	0	0	0	0	0	0	0

	K	L	M	N	O	P	Q	R	S
1	PAGE 2			SALES FORECAST					
2									
3									
4			JAN.	FEB.	MARCH	APRIL	MAY	JUNE	TOTAL
5									
6	INCOME FROM FORECASTED WORK								
7	PER INVOICE DATE								
8									
9	SALES NAME								
10	*								
11	*								0
12	*								0
13	*								0
14	*								0
15	*								0
16	*								0
17	*								0
18	*								0
19	*								0
20	*								0
21	*								0
22	*								0
23	*								0
24	*								0
25									
26	TOTAL		0	0	0	0	0	0	0
27									
28									
29	ASSUMPTION — WE WILL RECEIVE PAYMENT 2 MONTHS AFTER SALE								
30									
31	OPENING BALANCES (DEBTORS)								
32									
33									
34	SALES								
35									
36	FROM ABOVE								
37									
38									
39	SALES				0	0	0	0	
40									
41	TOTALS TO CASH -								
42	FLOW STATEMENT		0	0	0	0	0	0	0

	V	W	X	Y	Z	AA	AB	AC	AD
1	PAGE 3								
2					CASH FLOW FORECAST				
3									
4									
5				JAN.	FEB.	MARCH	APRIL	MAY	JUNE	TOTAL
6									
7									
8	INCOME..........			0	0	0	0	0	0	0
9									
10									
11	TOTAL			0	0	0	0	0	0	0
12									
13									
14	OUTGOINGS								
15									
16									
17	OFFICE RENTAL			....	....	....	....	....	....	0
18	RATES			....	....	....	....	....	....	0
19	SALARIES			0	0	0	0	0	0	0
20				....	....	....	....	....	....	
21	POST/STAT			....	....	....	....	....	....	0
22	TELEPHONE			....	....	....	....	....	....	0
23	CAR EXPENSES			....	....	....	....	....	....	0
24	CAPITAL EQUIP.			....	....	....	....	....	....	0
25	MISC. EXPENSES			....	....	....	....	....	....	0
26									
27									
28	TOTAL			0	0	0	0	0	0	0
29									
30	DEFICIT			0	0	0	0	0	0	0
31	OPENING								
32	BANK BAL.			....	0	0	0	0	0	0
33									
34									
35	CLOSING								
36	BANK BAL.			0	0	0	0	0	0	0
37									

TEMPLATE FOR STAFF / SALES / CASHFLOW

```
>I54:@SUM(C54...H54
>H54:+H51+H52
>G54:+G51+G52
>F54:+F51+F52
>E54:+E51+E52
>D54:+D51+D52
>C54:+C51+C52
>B54:/FR"TOTAL
>I53:/-
>H53:/-
>G53:/-
>F53:/-
>E53:/-
>D53:/-
>C53:/-
>B53:/-
>A53:/-
```

```
>I52:@SUM(C52...H52
>H52:+G40-G51
>G52:+F40-F51
>F52:+E40-E51
>E52:+D40-D51
>D52:+C40-C51
>C52:/FR"....
>B52:"IC
>A52:"PAYE & N
>I51:@SUM(C51...H51
>H51:@SUM(H40/3*2)
>G51:@SUM(G40/3*2)
>F51:@SUM(F40/3*2)
>E51:@SUM(E40/3*2)
>D51:@SUM(D40/3*2)
>C51:@SUM(C40/3*2)
>B51:"  COSTS
```

```
>B50:"OYMENT
>A50:"NET EMPL
>F48:"TS
>E48:"MENT COS
>D48:"L EMPLOY
>C48:" OF TOTA
>B48:"    1/3
>E47:"E
>D47:"C WILL B
>C47:"E AND NI
>B47:"ON - PAY
>A47:"ASSUMPTI
>AM46:/F*
>AL46:/F*
>AK46:/F*
>AJ46:/F*
>AI46:/F*
>AH46:/F*
>AG46:/F*
>AF46:/F*
>AE46:/F*
>AD46:/F*
>AC46:/F*
>AB46:/F*
>AA46:/F*
>Z46:/F*
>Y46:/F*
>C46:"-
>B46:"————
>A46:/—
>C45:"T
>B45:"W EXTRAC
>A45:"CASH FLO
>AM43:/F*
>AL43:/F*
>AK43:/F*
>AJ43:/F*
>S42:@SUM(M42...R42
>R42:+R34+R39
>Q42:+Q34+Q39
>P42:+P34+P39
>O42:+O34+O39
>N42:+N34+N39
>M42:+M34+M39
>L42:"TATEMENT
>K42:"  FLOW S
>H42:@COUNT(B9...B10)+@COUNT(B13...B15)+H19+@COUNT(B28...B30)+H32
>G42:@COUNT(B9...B10)+@COUNT(B13...B15)+G19+@COUNT(B28...B30)+G32
>F42:@COUNT(B9...B10)+@COUNT(B13...B15)+F19+@COUNT(B28...B30)+F32
>E42:@COUNT(B9...B10)+@COUNT(B13...B15)+E19+@COUNT(B28...B30)+E32
>D42:@COUNT(B9...B10)+@COUNT(B13...B15)+D19+@COUNT(B28...B30)+D32
>C42:@COUNT(B9...B10)+@COUNT(B13...B15)+C19+@COUNT(B28...B30)+C32
>B42:"AFF NO'S
>A42:"TOTAL ST
>L41:"O CASH
>K41:"TOTALS T
>S40:"/—
>R40:"/—
>Q40:"/—
>P40:"/—
>O40:"/—
>N40:"/—
>M40:"/—
>I40:+I35+I38
>H40:+H35+H38
>G40:+G35+G38
>F40:+F35+F38
>E40:+E35+E38
>D40:+D35+D38
>C40:+C35+C38
>B40:" TOTAL
>A40:/FR"GRAND
>R39:+P26
>Q39:+O26
>P39:+N26
>O39:+M26
>K39:"SALES
>I39:/-=
>H39:/-=
>G39:/-=
>F39:/-=
>E39:/-=
>D39:/-=
>C39:/-=
>B39:/-=
>A39:/-=
>I38:@SUM(C38...H38
>H38:@SUM(H35*B37)
>G38:@SUM(G35*B37)
>F38:@SUM(F35*B37)
>E38:@SUM(E35*B37)
>D38:@SUM(D35*B37)
>C38:@SUM(C35*B37)
>B38:"'S N.I.C
>A38:"EMPLOYER
>AD37:/—
>AC37:/—
>AB37:/—
>AA37:/—
>Z37:/—
>Y37:/—
>X37:/—
>W37:/—
>V37:/—
>L37:"—
>K37:/—
>B37:/FG.13
>A37:"NIC AV
>AD36:@SUM(AD30,AD32
>AC36:@SUM(AC30,AC32
>AB36:@SUM(AB30,AB32
>AA36:@SUM(AA30,AA32
>Z36:@SUM(Z30,Z32
>Y36:@SUM(Y30,Y32
>X36:@SUM(X30,X32
>W36:"NK BAL.
>V36:/FR"BA
>L36:"VE
>K36:"FROM ABO
>V35:"CLOSING
>I35:@SUM(I9...I33)
>H35:@SUM(H9...H10,H13...H17,H21,H28...H30,H33
>G35:@SUM(G9...G10,G13...G17,G21,G28...G30,G33
>F35:@SUM(F9...F10,F13...F17,F21,F28...F30,F33
```

```
>E35:@SUM(E9...E10,E13...E17,E21,E28...E30,E33
>D35:@SUM(D9...D10,D13...D17,D21,D28...D30,D33
>C35:@SUM(C9...C10,C13 .C17,C21,C28...C30,C33
>B35:"LARIES
>A35:"TOTAL SA
>AD34:/-
>AC34:/-
>AB34:/-
>AA34:/-
>Z34:/-
>Y34:/-
>X34:/-
>W34:/-
>V34:/-
>K34:"SALES
>I34:/-
>H34:/-
>G34:/-
>F34:/-
>E34:/-
>D34:/-
>C34:/-
>B34:/-
>A34:/-
>I33:@SUM(C33...H33
>H33:@SUM(B33*H32)
>G33:@SUM(B33*G32)
>F33:@SUM(B33*F32)
>E33:@SUM(B33*E32)
>D33:@SUM(B33*D32)
>C33:@SUM(B33*C32)
>B33:250
>A33:"TYPIST #
>AD32:+X32
>AC32:+AB36
>AB32:+AA36
>AA32:+Z36
>Z32:+Y36
>Y32:+X36
>X32:/FR"....
>W32:"NK BAL.
>V32:/FR"BA
>L32:/-
>K32:/-
>H32:+G32
>G32:+F32
>F32:+E32
>E32:+D32
>D32:+C32
>C32:0
>B32:"O'S
>A32:"TYPIST N
>V31:"OPENING
>N31:"S)
>M31:" (DEBTOR
>L31:"BALANCES
>K31:"OPENING
>B31:"PER PERS
>AD30:+AD11-AD28
>AC30:+AC11-AC28
>AB30:+AB11-AB28
>AA30:+AA11-AA28
>Z30:+Z11-Z28
>Y30:+Y11-Y28
>X30:+X11-X28
>W30:"DEFICIT
>I30:@SUM(C30...H30
>H30:+G30
>G30:+F30
>F30:+E30
>E30:+D30
>D30:+C30
>C30:+B30
>A30:"NAME
>AD29:/-
>AC29:/-
>AB29:/-
>AA29:/-
>Z29:/-
>Y29:/-
>X29:/-
>W29:/-
>V29:/-
>Q29:"TER SALE
>P29:"ONTHS AF
>O29:"MENT 2 M
>N29:"EIVE PAY
>M29:"WILL REC
>L29:"ON - WE
>K29:"ASSUMPTI
>I29:@SUM(C29...H29
>H29:+G29
>G29:+F29
>F29:+E29
>E29:+D29
>D29:+C29
>C29:+B29
>B29:/FR"....
>A29:"NAME
>AD28:@SUM(AD17...AD26)
>AC28:@SUM(AC17...AC26)
>AB28:@SUM(AB17...AB26)
>AA28:@SUM(AA17...AA26)
>Z28:@SUM(Z17...Z26)
>Y28:@SUM(Y17...Y26)
>X28:@SUM(X17...X26)
>V28:"TOTAL
>I28:@SUM(C28...H28
>H28:+G28
>G28:+F28
>F28:+E28
>E28:+D28
>D28:+C28
>C28:+B28
>B28:/FR"....
>A28:"NAME
>AD27:/-
>AC27:/-
>AB27:/-
>AA27:/-
>Z27:/-
>Y27:/-
>X27:/-
>W27:/-
```

```
>V27:/-
>S27:/-
>R27:/-
>Q27:/-
>P27:/-
>O27:/-
>N27:/-
>M27:/-
>L27:/-
>K27:/-
>C27:"--
>B27:/-
>A27:/-
>S26:@SUM(S10...S24
>R26:@SUM(R10...R24
>Q26:@SUM(Q10...Q24
>P26:@SUM(P10...P24
>O26:@SUM(O10...O24
>N26:@SUM(N10...N24
>M26:@SUM(M10...M24
>K26:"TOTAL
>C26:"TAFF
>B26:"RATION S
>A26:"ADMINIST
>AD25:@SUM(X25...AC25
>AC25:/FR"....
>AB25:/FR"....
>AA25:/FR"....
>Z25:/FR"....
>Y25:/FR"....
>X25:/FR"....
>W25:"PENSES
>V25:"MISC. EX
>S25:/-=
>R25:/-=
>Q25:/-=
>P25:/-=
>O25:/-=
>N25:/-=
>M25:/-=
>L25:/-=
>K25:/-=
>I25:/-
>H25:/-
>G25:/-
>F25:/-
>E25:/-
>D25:/-
>C25:/-
>B25:/-
>A25:/-
>AD24:@SUM(X24...AC24
>AC24:/FR"....
>AB24:/FR"....
>AA24:/FR"....
>Z24:/FR"....
>Y24:/FR"....
>X24:/FR"....
>W24:"EQUIP.
>V24:"CAPITAL
>S24:@SUM(M24...R24
>L24:/F$
```

```
>K24:"*
>H24:@COUNT(B9...B10)+H19+@COUNT(B13...B17
>G24:@COUNT(B9...B10)+G19+@COUNT(B13...B17
>F24:@COUNT(B9...B10)+F19+@COUNT(B13...B17
>E24:@COUNT(B9...B10)+E19+@COUNT(B13...B17
>D24:@COUNT(B9...B10)+D19+@COUNT(B13...B17
>C24:@COUNT(B9...B10)+C19+@COUNT(B13...B17
>A24:" STAFF
>AD23:@SUM(X23...AC23
>AC23:/FR"....
>AB23:/FR"....
>AA23:/FR"....
>Z23:/FR"....
>Y23:/FR"....
>X23:/FR"....
>W23:"NSES
>V23:"CAR EXPE
>S23:@SUM(M23...R23
>L23:/F$
>K23:"*
>C23:"AL
>B23:"OFESSION
>A23:"TOTAL PR
>AD22:@SUM(X22...AC22
>AC22:/FR"....
>AB22:/FR"....
>AA22:/FR"....
>Z22:/FR"....
>Y22:/FR"....
>X22:/FR"....
>W22:"E
>V22:"TELEPHON
>S22:@SUM(M22...R22
>L22:/F$
>K22:"*
>I22:/-
>H22:/-
>G22:/-
>F22:/-
>E22:/-
>D22:/-
>C22:/-
>B22:/-
>A22:/-
>AD21:@SUM(X21...AC21
>AC21:/FR"....
>AB21:/FR"....
>AA21:/FR"....
>Z21:/FR"....
>Y21:/FR"....
>X21:/FR"....
>W21:"T
>V21:"POST/STA
>S21:@SUM(M21...R21
>L21:/F$
>K21:"*
>I21:@SUM(C21...H21
>H21:@SUM(B21*H19)
>G21:@SUM(B21*G19)
>F21:@SUM(B21*F19)
>E21:@SUM(B21*E19)
>D21:@SUM(B21*D19)
```

```
>C21:@SUM(B21*C19)
>B21:@IF(@ISERROR(B20),0,B20)
>A21:"SENIOR #
>AC20:/FR"....
>AB20:/FR"....
>AA20:/FR"....
>Z20:/FR"....
>Y20:/FR"....
>X20:/FR"....
>S20:@SUM(M20...R20
>L20:/F$
>K20:"*
>B20:@AVERAGE(B13...B17
>AD19:@SUM(X19...AC19
>AC19:+H54
>AB19:+G54
>AA19:+F54
>Z19:+E54
>Y19:+D54
>X19:+C54
>V19:"SALARIES
>S19:@SUM(M19...R19
>L19:/F$
>K19:"*
>H19:+G19
>G19:+F19
>F19:+E19
>E19:+D19
>D19:+C19
>C19:0
>B19:"AFF NO'S
>A19:"EXTRA ST
>AD18:@SUM(X18...AC18
>AC18:/FR"....
>AB18:/FR"....
>AA18:/FR"....
>Z18:/FR"....
>Y18:/FR"....
>X18:/FR"....
>V18:"RATES
>S18:@SUM(M18...R18
>L18:/F$
>K18:"*
>AD17:@SUM(X17...AC17
>AC17:/FR"....
>AB17:/FR"....
>AA17:/FR"....
>Z17:/FR"....
>Y17:/FR"....
>X17:/FR"....
>W17:"ENTAL
>V17:"OFFICE R
>S17:@SUM(M17...R17
>L17:/F$
>K17:"*
>I17:@SUM(C17...H17
>H17:+G17
>G17:+F17
>F17:+E17
>E17:+D17
>D17:+C17
>C17:+B17
>B17:/FR"....
>A17:"NAME
>S16:@SUM(M16...R16
>L16:/F$
>K16:"*
>I16:@SUM(C16...H16
>H16:+G16
>G16:+F16
>F16:+E16
>E16:+D16
>D16:+C16
>C16:+B16
>B16:/FR"....
>A16:"NAME
>W15:"—
>V15:/—
>S15:@SUM(M15...R15
>L15:/F$
>K15:"*
>I15:@SUM(C15...H15
>H15:+G15
>G15:+F15
>F15:+E15
>E15:+D15
>D15:+C15
>C15:+B15
>B15:/FR"....
>A15:"NAME
>W14:"S
>V14:"OUTGOING
>S14:@SUM(M14...R14
>L14:/F$
>K14:"*
>I14:@SUM(C14...H14
>H14:+G14
>G14:+F14
>F14:+E14
>E14:+D14
>D14:+C14
>C14:+B14
>B14:/FR"....
>A14:"NAME
>S13:@SUM(M13...R13
>L13:/F$
>K13:"*
>I13:@SUM(C13...H13
>H13:+G13
>G13:+F13
>F13:+E13
>E13:+D13
>D13:+C13
>C13:+B13
>B13:/FR"....
>A13:"NAME
>AD12:/—
>AC12:/—
>AB12:/—
>AA12:/—
>Z12:/—
>Y12:/—
>X12:/—
>W12:/—
```

```
>V12:/-
>S12:@SUM(M12...R12
>L12:/F$
>K12:"*
>B12:"AFF
>A12:"SALES ST
>AD11:@SUM(AD8...AD9
>AC11:@SUM(AC8...AC9
>AB11:@SUM(AB8...AB9
>AA11:@SUM(AA8...AA9
>Z11:@SUM(Z8...Z9
>Y11:@SUM(Y8...Y9
>X11:@SUM(X8...X9
>V11:"TOTAL
>S11:@SUM(M11...R11
>L11:/F$
>K11:"*
>AD10:/-
>AC10:/-
>AB10:/-
>AA10:/-
>Z10:/-
>Y10:/-
>X10:/-
>L10:/F$
>K10:"*
>I10:@SUM(C10...H10
>H10:+G10
>G10:+F10
>F10:+E10
>E10:+D10
>D10:+C10
>C10:+B10
>B10:/FR"....
>A10:"NAME
>L9:"NAME
>K9:/FR"SALES
>I9:@SUM(C9...H9
>H9:+G9
>G9:+F9
>F9:+E9
>E9:+D9
>D9:+C9
>C9:+B9
>B9:/FR"....
>A9:"NAME
>AD8:@SUM(X8...AC8
>AC8:+R42
>AB8:+Q42
>AA8:+P42
>Z8:+O42
>Y8:+N42
>X8:+M42
>W8:/-.
>V8:"INCOME..
>S8:/-
>R8:/-
>Q8:/-
>P8:/-
>O8:/-
>N8:/-
>M8:/-
>L8:/-
>K8:/-
>B8:"S
>A8:"DIRECTOR
>M7:"ICE DATE
>L7:"PER INVO
>B7:" SALARY
>AD6:/-
>AC6:/-
>AB6:/-
>AA6:/-
>Z6:/-
>Y6:/-
>X6:/-
>N6:"ORK
>M6:"CASTED W
>L6:"ROM FORE
>K6:"INCOME F
>B6:"  BASIC
>AD5:/FR"TOTAL
>AC5:/FR" JUNE
>AB5:/FR" MAY
>AA5:/FR"APRIL
>Z5:/FR"MARCH
>Y5:/FR" FEB.
>X5:/FR" JAN.
>S5:/-
>R5:/-
>Q5:/-
>P5:/-
>O5:/-
>N5:/-
>M5:/-
>L5:/-
>K5:/-
>I5:/-
>H5:/-
>G5:/-
>F5:/-
>E5:/-
>D5:/-
>C5:/-
>B5:/-
>A5:/-
>S4:/FR"TOTAL
>R4:/FR" JUNE
>Q4:/FR" MAY
>P4:/FR"APRIL
>O4:/FR"MARCH
>N4:/FR" FEB.
>M4:/FR" JAN.
>L4:/FG
>I4:/FR"TOTAL
>H4:/FR"JUNE
>G4:/FR"MAY
>F4:/FR"APRIL
>E4:/FR"MARCH
>D4:/FR"FEB.
>C4:/FR"JAN.
>B4:/FG"  DD.MM
```

```
>A4:"PREPARED
>Z3:"==
>Y3:/-=
>X3:/-=
>W3:/FL
>V3:/FG
>C3:/FG"  ****.**
>B3:"L YEAR
>A3:"FINANCIA
>Z2:"ST
>Y2:"W FORECA
>X2:"CASH FLO
>V2:/-
>P2:/-
>O2:/FR"---
>M2:/FG
>K2:/-
>F2:/-
>E2:/-
A2:/-
>V1:"PAGE 3
>P1:"FORECAST
>O1:/FR"SALES
>K1:"PAGE 2
>F1:"NT COSTS
>E1:"EMPLOYME
>A1:"PAGE 1
/W1
/GOC
/GRM
/GFI
/GC8
/X>A1:>A6:/TH
/X!/X>A1:>A1:
```

	A	B	F	G	H	I	J	K	L	M	N	O	
1													
2		EXTENDED TRIAL BALANCE			MONTH – MONTH		YEAR						
3													
4							CREDITORS						
5		DESCRIPTION	N/L		ADJUSTMENTS		& DEBTORS			PROFIT	BALANCE		
6	N/LEDGER		BALANCES				ACCRUALS &			& LOSS	SHEET		
7	REFERENCE						PRE-⟨=⟩PAYMENTS						
8													
9			DR	CR	DR	CR	DR	CR	DR	CR	DR	CR	
10			+	–	+	–	+	–	+	–	+	–	
11	101	MOTOR VEHICLES COST									0.00	0.00	TRUE
12	102	OFF&F COST									0.00	0.00	TRUE
13	103	DEPRECIATION									0.00	0.00	TRUE
14	104	DEPRECIATION									0.00	0.00	TRUE
15											0.00	0.00	TRUE
16	201	BANK ACCOUNT NO. 1									0.00	0.00	TRUE
17	202	BANK ACCOUNT NO. 2									0.00	0.00	TRUE
18	203	BUILDING SOCIETY									0.00	0.00	TRUE
19	204	CASH IN HAND									0.00	0.00	TRUE
20													TRUE
21	301	BOUGHT LEDGER					0.00						TRUE
22	302	SALES LEDGER						0.00					TRUE
23	303	V.A.T.						0.00					TRUE
24	304	PAYE – N.I.C.						0.00					TRUE
25	305	NET PAY											TRUE
26	306	HP CAR 1									0.00	0.00	TRUE
27	307	HP CAR 2									0.00	0.00	TRUE
28	308	WORK IN PROGRESS											TRUE
29													TRUE
30													TRUE
31													TRUE
32	401	SHARE CAPITAL									0.00	0.00	TRUE
33	402	RESERVES									0.00	0.00	TRUE
34	403	HP INTEREST SUSPENCE									0.00	0.00	TRUE
35	404	BANK LOAN									0.00	0.00	TRUE
36													TRUE
37	501	SALES – TYPE 1								0.00			TRUE
38	502	SALES – TYPE 2								0.00			TRUE
39	503	SALES – TYPE 3								0.00			TRUE
40	504	SALES – TYPE 4								0.00			TRUE
41	505	SALES – TYPE 5								0.00			TRUE
42	506	SALES – OTHER								0.00			TRUE
43													TRUE
44	601	CONSULTANCY FEES							0.00				TRUE
45	602	SUB – CONTRACT							0.00				TRUE
46	603	SALARIES ADMIN							0.00				TRUE
47	604	SALARIES PRODUCTIVE							0.00				TRUE
48	605	DIRECTORS REMUNERATION							0.00				TRUE
49	606	RECRUITMENT							0.00				TRUE
50	607	RENT							0.00				TRUE
51	608	RATES							0.00				TRUE
52	609	HEAT AND LIGHT							0.00				TRUE
53	610	TELEPHONE & TELEX							0.00				TRUE
54	611	PRINTING AND STATIONERY							0.00				TRUE
55	612	POSTAGE							0.00				TRUE
56													TRUE
57													
58													
59													
60													

	A	B	C	D	E	F	G	H	I	J	K	L	M	N	O
67			EXTENDED TRIAL BALANCE												
68															
69									CREDITORS						
70			DESCRIPTION			N/L		ADJUSTMENTS	& DEBTORS			PROFIT		BALANCE	
71	N/LEDGER					BALANCES			ACCRUALS &			& LOSS		SHEET	
72	REFERENCE								PRE- ⟨=⟩ PAYMENTS						
73															
74						DR	CR	DR	CR	DR	CR	DR	CR	DR	CR
75						+	−	+	−	+	−	+	−	+	−
76	613	ADVERTISING & EXHIBS										0.00			
77	614	PHOTOCOPIER										0.00				TRUE
78	615	COMPUTERS										0.00				TRUE
79	616	REPAIRS & RENEWALS										0.00				TRUE
80	617	MOTOR EXPENSES										0.00				TRUE
81	618	TRAVEL - UK										0.00				TRUE
82	619	TRAVEL - FOREIGN										0.00				TRUE
83	620	SUBSISTENCE & ACCOM.										0.00				TRUE
84	621	ENTERTAINING - UK										0.00				TRUE
85	622	ENTERTAINING - FOREIGN										0.00				TRUE
86	623											0.00				TRUE
87	624	AUDIT & ACCOUNTANCY										0.00				TRUE
88	625	LEGAL FEES										0.00				TRUE
89	626	LEASING										0.00				TRUE
90	627	HP INTEREST										0.00				TRUE
91	628	BANK CHARGES & INTEREST										0.00				TRUE
92	629	DEPRECIATION MOTOR CARS										0.00				TRUE
93	630	DEPRECIATION - OFF&F										0.00				TRUE
94	631	LOAN INTEREST										0.00				TRUE
95	632											0.00				TRUE
96	633	SUNDRY										0.00				TRUE
97	634	SUBSCRIPTIONS										0.00				TRUE
98	635	BOOKS, PAPERS ETC										0.00				TRUE
99																TRUE
100																TRUE
101	700	INSURANCE MOTOR										0.00				TRUE
102	701	INSURANCE OFFICE										0.00				TRUE
103	702	INSURANCE SICKNESS										0.00				TRUE
104	703	INSURANCE PENSION										0.00				TRUE
105																TRUE
106															
107															
108						0.00	0.00	0.00	0.00	0.00	0.00	0.00	0.00	0.00	0.00
109															
110		DEBTORS												0.00	
111		CREDITORS													0.00
112															
113															
114															
115		PROFIT/LOSS										0.00	0.00	0.00	0.00
116															
117															
118															
119															
120															
121															
122												0.00	0.00	0.00	0.00
123													0.00		0.00

(Page 3 to right of page 1)

```
        Q        R        S        T
 1      TRADING AND PROFIT AND LOSS ACCOUNT
 2      --------------------------------
 3                                      UNAUDITED
 4                                      =========
 5
 6                                 YEAR
 7                                TO DATE
 8                                --------
 9
10      Sales                             0
11      Stock and Opening WIP             0
12      Closing WIP                       0
13
14                                --------
15                                        0
16      OVERHEADS
17      ---------
18      Directors Remuneration            0
19      Salaries                          0
20      Sub-Contract                      0
21      Recruitment                       0
22      Rent, Rates and SERVICES          0
23      Telephone and TeLEX               0
24      Motor Expenses                    0
25      Travel & EntertaINMENT            0
26      Subsistance and ACCOM.            0
27      Leasing                           0
28      Printing Post anD STAT.           0
29      Photocopier      )                0
30      COMPUTERS        )                0
31      Books, Subs. Papers ETC           0
32      Audit and AccounTANCY             0
33      Legal Fees                        0
34      Repairs and RenoVATIONS           0
35      Advertising and EXHIBS            0
36      Sundry                            0
37      InsurancES                        0
38      Depreciation                      0
39      HP Interest                       0
40      Bank Charges & INTEREST           0
41      BANK LOAN INTEREST                0
42
43
44                                --------
45                                        0
46
47
48      Net Loss/Profit.......            0
```

TEMPLATE FOR EXTENDED TRIAL BALANCE

```
>N123:@IF(M122=N122,@TRUE,M122-N122)
>L123:@IF(K122=L122,@TRUE,K122-L122)
>N122:@SUM(N108...N120
>M122:@SUM(M108...M120
>L122:@SUM(L108...L120
>K122:@SUM(K108...K120
>N121:/-
>M121:/-
>L121:/-
>K121:/-
>N115:+K115
>M115:+L115
>L115:@IF(K108
>L108,K108-L108,0)
>K115:@IF(K108<L108-K108,0)
>C115:"OSS
>B115:"PROFIT/L
>N111:+I108
>C111:"S
>B111:"CREDITOR
>M110:+J108
>B110:"DEBTORS
>J109:/-
>I109:/-
>H109:/-
>G109:/-
>F109:/-
>E109:/-
>N108:@SUM(N6...N106
>M108:@SUM(M6...M106
>L108:@SUM(J6...L106
>K108:@SUM(K6...K106
>J108:@SUM(J6...J106
>I108:@SUM(I6...I106
>H108:@SUM(H6...H106
>G108:@SUM(J6...G106
>F108:@SUM(F6...F106
>E108:@SUM(E6...E106
>N107:/-
>M107:/-
>L107:/-
>K107:/-
>J107:/-
>I107:/-
>H107:/-
>G107:/-
>F107:/-
>E107:/-
```

```
>O105:@IF(@SUM(E105-F105+G105-H105+I105-J105)=@SUM(K105-L105+M105-N105),@TRUE,@FALSE)
>O104:@IF(@SUM(E104-F104+G104-H104+I104-J104)=@SUM(K104-L104+M104-N104),@TRUE,@FALSE)
>L104:/F$
>K104:/F$@IF(E104-F104+G104-H104+I104-J104>0,E104-F104+G104-H104+I104-J104,0)
>D104:"N
>C104:"E PENSIO
>B104:"INSURANC
>A104:/FL+A103+1
>O103:@IF(@SUM(E103-F103+G103-H103+I103-J103)=@SUM(K103-L103+M103-N103),@TRUE,@FALSE)
>L103:/F$
>K103:/F$@IF(E103-F103+G103-H103+I103-J103>0,E103-F103+G103-H103+I103-J103,0)
>D103:"SS
>C103:"E SICKNE
>B103:"INSURANC
>A103:/FL+A102+1
>O102:@IF(@SUM(E102-F102+G102-H102+I102-J102)=@SUM(K102-L102+M102-N102),@TRUE,@FALSE)
>L102:/F$
>K102:/F$@IF(E102-F102+G102-H102+I102-J102>0,E102-F102+G102-H102+I102-J102,0)
>C102:"E OFFICE
>B102:"INSURANC
>A102:/FL+A101+1
>O101:@IF(@SUM(E101-F101+G101-H101+I101-J101)=@SUM(K101-L101+M101-N101),@TRUE,@FALSE)
>L101:/F$
>K101:/F$@IF(E101-F101+G101-H101+I101-J101>0,E101-F101+G101-H101+I101-J101,0)
>C101:"E MOTOR
>B101:"INSURANC
>A101:/FL700
>O100:@IF(@SUM(E100-F100+G100-H100+I100-J100)=@SUM(K100-L100+M100-N100),@TRUE,@FALSE)
>L100:/F$
>O99:@IF(@SUM(E99-F99+G99-H99+I99-J99)=@SUM(K99-L99+M99-N99),@TRUE,@FALSE)
>L99:/F$
>O98:@IF(@SUM(E98-F98+G98-H98+I98-J98)=@SUM(K98-L98+M98-N98),@TRUE,@FALSE)
>L98:/F$
>K98:/F$@IF(E98-F98+G98-H98+I98-J98>0,E98-F98+G98-H98+I98-J98,0)
>D98:"C
>C98:"APERS ET
>B98:"BOOKS, P
>A98:/FL+A97+1
>O97:@IF(@SUM(E97-F97+G97-H97+I97-J97)=@SUM(K97-L97+M97-N97),@TRUE,@FALSE)
>L97:/F$
>K97:/F$@IF(E97-F97+G97-H97+I97-J97>0,E97-F97+G97-H97+I97-J97,0)
>C97:"TIONS
>B97:"SUBSCRIP
>A97:/FL+A96+1
>O96:@IF(@SUM(E96-F96+G96-H96+I96-J96)=@SUM(K96-L96+M96-N96),@TRUE,@FALSE)
>L96:/F$
>K96:/F$@IF(E96-F96+G96-H96+I96-J96>0,E96-F96+G96-H96+I96-J96,0)
>B96:"SUNDRY
>A96:/FL+A95+1
>O95:@IF(@SUM(E95-F95+G95-H95+I95-J95)=@SUM(K95-L95+M95-N95),@TRUE,@FALSE)
>L95:/F$
>K95:/F$@IF(E95-F95+G95-H95+I95-J95>0,E95-F95+G95-H95+I95-J95,0)
>A95:/FL+A94+1
>O94:@IF(@SUM(E94-F94+G94-H94+I94-J94)=@SUM(K94-L94+M94-N94),@TRUE,@FALSE)
>L94:/F$
>K94:/F$@IF(E94-F94+G94-H94+I94-J94>0,E94-F94+G94-H94+I94-J94,0)
>C94:"EREST
>B94:"LOAN INT
>A94:/FL+A93+1
>O93:@IF(@SUM(E93-F93+G93-H93+I93-J93)=@SUM(K93-L93+M93-N93),@TRUE,@FALSE)
>L93:/F$
```

```
>K93:/F$@IF(E93-F93+G93-H93+I93-J93>0,E93-F93+G93-H93+I93-J93,0)
>D93:"FF&F
>C93:"TION - O
>B93:"DEPRECIA
>A93:/FL+A92+1
>O92:@IF(@SUM(E92-F92+G92-H92+I92-J92)=@SUM(K92-L92+M92-N92),@TRUE,@FALSE)
>L92:/F$
>K92:/F$@IF(E92-F92+G92-H92+I92-J92>0,E92-F92+G92-H92+I92-J92,0)
>D92:"OR CARS
>C92:"TION MOT
>B92:"DEPRECIA
>A92:/FL+A91+1
>O91:@IF(@SUM(E91-F91+G91-H91+I91-J91)=@SUM(K91-L91+M91-N91),@TRUE,@FALSE)
>L91:/F$
>K91:/F$@IF(E91-F91+G91-H91+I91-J91>0,E91-F91+G91-H91+I91-J91,0)
>D91:"NTEREST
>C91:"RGES & I
>B91:"BANK CHA
>A91:/FL+A90+1
>O90:@IF(@SUM(E90-F90+G90-H90+I90-J90)=@SUM(K90-L90+M90-N90),@TRUE,@FALSE)
>L90:/F$
>K90:/F$@IF(E90-F90+G90-H90+I90-J90>0,E90-F90+G90-H90+I90-J90,0)
>C90:"EST
>B90:"HP INTER
>A90:/FL+A89+1
>O89:@IF(@SUM(E89-F89+G89-H89+I89-J89)=@SUM(K89-L89+M89-N89),@TRUE,@FALSE)
>L89:/F$
>K89:/F$@IF(E89-F89+G89-H89+I89-J89>0,E89-F89+G89-H89+I89-J89,0)
>B89:"LEASING
>A89:/FL+A88+1
>O88:@IF(@SUM(E88-F88+G88-H88+I88-J88)=@SUM(K88-L88+M88-N88),@TRUE,@FALSE)
>L88:/F$
>K88:/F$@IF(E88-F88+G88-H88+I88-J88>0,E88-F88+G88-H88+I88-J88,0)
>C88:"ES
>B88:"LEGAL FE
>A88:/FL+A87+1
>O87:@IF(@SUM(E87-F87+G87-H87+I87-J87)=@SUM(K87-L87+M87-N87),@TRUE,@FALSE)
>L87:/F$
>K87:/F$@IF(E87-F87+G87-H87+I87-J87>0,E87-F87+G87-H87+I87-J87,0)
>D87:"NCY
>C87:"ACCOUNTA
>B87:"AUDIT &
>A87:/FL+A86+1
>O86:@IF(@SUM(E86-F86+G86-H86+I86-J86)=@SUM(K86-L86+M86-N86),@TRUE,@FALSE)
>L86:/F$
>K86:/F$@IF(E86-F86+G86-H86+I86-J86>0,E86-F86+G86-H86+I86-J86,0)
>A86:/FL+A85+1
>O85:@IF(@SUM(E85-F85+G85-H85+I85-J85)=@SUM(K85-L85+M85-N85),@TRUE,@FALSE)
>L85:/F$
>K85:/F$@IF(E85-F85+G85-H85+I85-J85>0,E85-F85+G85-H85+I85-J85,0)
>D85:"OREIGN
>C85:"NING - F
>B85:"ENTERTAI
>A85:/FL+A84+1
>O84:@IF(@SUM(E84-F84+G84-H84+I84-J84)=@SUM(K84-L84+M84-N84),@TRUE,@FALSE)
>L84:/F$
>K84:/F$@IF(E84-F84+G84-H84+I84-J84>0,E84-F84+G84-H84+I84-J84,0)
>D84:"K
>C84:"NING - U
>B84:"ENTERTAI
>A84:/FL+A83+1
```

```
>O83:@IF(@SUM(E83-F83+G83-H83+I83-J83)=@SUM(K83-L83+M83-N83),@TRUE,@FALSE)
>L83:/F$
>K83:/F$@IF(E83-F83+G83-H83+I83-J83>0,E83-F83+G83-H83+I83-J83,0)
>D83:"COM.
>C83:"NCE & AC
>B83:"SUBSISTE
>A83:/FL+A82+1
>O82:@IF(@SUM(E82-F82+G82-H82+I82-J82)=@SUM(K82-L82+M82-N82),@TRUE,@FALSE)
>L82:/F$
>K82:/F$@IF(E82-F82+G82-H82+I82-J82>0,E82-F82+G82-H82+I82-J82,0)
>C82:" FOREIGN
>B82:"TRAVEL -
>A82:/FL+A81+1
>O81:@IF(@SUM(E81-F81+G81-H81+I81-J81)=@SUM(K81-L81+M81-N81),@TRUE,@FALSE)
>L81:/F$
>K81:/F$@IF(E81-F81+G81-H81+I81-J81>0,E81-F81+G81-H81+I81-J81,0)
>C81:" UK
>B81:"TRAVEL -
>A81:/FL+A80+1
>O80:@IF(@SUM(E80-F80+G80-H80+I80-J80)=@SUM(K80-L80+M80-N80),@TRUE,@FALSE)
>L80:/F$
>K80:/F$@IF(E80-F80+G80-H80+I80-J80>0,E80-F80+G80-H80+I80-J80,0)
>C80:"PENSES
>B80:"MOTOR EX
>A80:/FL+A79+1
>O79:@IF(@SUM(E79-F79+G79-H79+I79-J79)=@SUM(K79-L79+M79-N79),@TRUE,@FALSE)
>L79:/F$
>K79:/F$@IF(E79-F79+G79-H79+I79-J79>0,E79-F79+G79-H79+I79-J79,0)
>D79:"LS
>C79:"& RENEWA
>B79:"REPAIRS
>A79:/FL+A78+1
>O78:@IF(@SUM(E78-F78+G78-H78+I78-J78)=@SUM(K78-L78+M78-N78),@TRUE,@FALSE)
>L78:/F$
>K78:/F$@IF(E78-F78+G78-H78+I78-J78>0,E78-F78+G78-H78+I78-J78,0)
>C78:"S
>B78:"COMPUTER
>A78:/FL+A77+1
>O77:@IF(@SUM(E77-F77+G77-H77+I77-J77)=@SUM(K77-L77+M77-N77),@TRUE,@FALSE)
>L77:/F$
>K77:/F$@IF(E77-F77+G77-H77+I77-J77>0,E77-F77+G77-H77+I77-J77,0)
>C77:"IER
>B77:"PHOTOCOP
>A77:/FL+A76+1
>L76:/F$
>K76:/F$@IF(E76-F76+G76-H76+I76-J76>0,E76-F76+G76-H76+I76-J76,0)
>D76:"HIBS
>C76:"ING & EX
>B76:"ADVERTIS
>A76:/FL613
>N75:"    -
>M75:"    +
>L75:"    -
>K75:"    +
>J75:"    -
>I75:"    +
>H75:"    -
>G75:"    +
>F75:"    -
>E75:"    +
>N74:/FR"    CR
>M74:/FR"    DR
>L74:/FR"    CR
>K74:/FR"    DR
>J74:/FR"    CR
>I74:/FR"    DR
>H74:/FR"    CR
>G74:/FR"    DR
>F74:/FR"    CR
>E74:/FR"    DR
>N73:/-
>M73:/-
>L73:/-
>K73:/-
>J73:/-
>I73:/-
>H73:/-
>G73:/-
>F73:/-
>E73:/-
>D73:/-
>C73:/-
>B73:/-
>A73:/-
>J72:/FR"PAYMENTS
>B72:"E
>A72:"REFERENCE
>N71:/FR"SHEET
>L71:"  & LOSS
>K71:" =
>J71:/FR"& PRE-
>I71:/FR"ACCRUALS
>H71:/FR
>F71:"NCES
>E71:/FR"BALA
>A71:/FL"N/LEDGER
>N70:/FL"ANCE
>M70:/FR"BAL
>L70:/FL"FIT
>K70:/FR"PRO
>J70:/FR"DEBTORS
>I70:/FR"ITORS &
>H70:/FL"TMENTS
>G70:/FR"ADJUS
>F70:/FL"L
>E70:/FR"N/
>C70:"PTION
>B70:"  DESCRI
>I69:/FR"CRED-
>F69:/F$
>E69:/F$
>F68:/F$
>E68:/F$
>D68:"----
>C68:/-
>B68:"----
>F67:/F$
>E67:/F$
>D67:"ALANCE
>C67:" TRIAL B
>B67:"EXTENDED
>F66:/F$
```

```
>E66:/F$
>F65:/F$
>E65:/F$
>F64:/F$
>E64:/F$
>F63:/F$
>E63:/F$
>F62:/F$
>E62:/F$
>N61:/-
>M61:/-
>L61:/-
>K61:/-
>J61:/-
>I61:/-
>H61:/-
>G61:/-
>F61:/-
>E61:/-
>D61:/-
>C61:/-
>B61:/-
>A61:/-
>N60:/F$
>M60:/F$
>L60:/F$
>K60:/F$
>J60:/F$
>I60:/F$
>F60:/F$
>E60:/F$
>N59:/F$
>M59:/F$
>L59:/F$
>K59:/F$
>J59:/F$
>I59:/F$
>F59:/F$
>E59:/F$
>N58:/F$
>M58:/F$
>L58:/F$
>K58:/F$
>J58:/F$
>I58:/F$
>F58:/F$
>E58:/F$
>N57:/F$
>M57:/F$
>L57:/F$
>K57:/F$
>J57:/F$
>I57:/F$
>F57:/F$
>E57:/F$
>O56:@IF(@SUM(E56-F56+G56-H56+I56-J56)=@SUM(K56-L56+M56-N56),@TRUE,@FALSE)
>N56:/F$
>M56:/F$
>L56:/F$
>K56:/F$
>J56:/F$
>I56:/F$
>H56:/FR
>G56:/FR
>F56:/F$
>E56:/F$
>O55:@IF(@SUM(E55-F55+G55-H55+I55-J55)=@SUM(K55-L55+M55-N55),@TRUE,@FALSE)
>N55:/F$
>M55:/F$
>L55:/F$
>K55:/F$@IF(E55-F55+G55-H55+I55-J55>0,E55-F55+G55-H55+I55-J55,0)
>J55:/F$
>I55:/F$
>H55:/F$
>G55:/F$
>F55:/F$
>E55:/F$
>B55:"POSTAGE
>A55:/FL+A54+1
>O54:@IF(@SUM(E54-F54+G54-H54+I54-J54)=@SUM(K54-L54+M54-N54),@TRUE,@FALSE)
>N54:/F$
>M54:/F$
>L54:/F$
>K54:/F$@IF(E54-F54+G54-H54+I54-J54>0,E54-F54+G54-H54+I54-J54,0)
>J54:/F$
>I54:/F$
>H54:/F$
>G54:/F$
>F54:/F$
>E54:/F$
>D54:"TIONERY
>C54:" AND STA
>B54:"PRINTING
>A54:/FL+A53+1
>O53:@IF(@SUM(E53-F53+G53-H53+I53-J53)=@SUM(K53-L53+M53-N53),@TRUE,@FALSE)
>N53:/F$
>M53:/F$
>L53:/F$
>K53:/F$@IF(E53-F53+G53-H53+I53-J53>0,E53-F53+G53-H53+I53-J53,0)
>J53:/F$
>I53:/F$
>H53:/F$
>G53:/F$
>F53:/F$
>E53:/F$
>D53:"X
>C53:"E & TELEX
>B53:"TELEPHON
>A53:/FL+A52+1
>O52:@IF(@SUM(E52-F52+G52-H52+I52-J52)=@SUM(K52-L52+M52-N52),@TRUE,@FALSE)
>N52:/F$
>M52:/F$
>L52:/F$
```

```
>K52:/F$@IF(E52-F52+G52-H52+I52-J52>0,E52-F52+G52-H52+I52-J52,0)
>J52:/F$
>I52:/F$
>H52:/F$
>G52:/F$
>F52:/F$
>E52:/F$
>C52:" LIGHT
>B52:"HEAT AND
>A52:/FL+A51+1
>U51:/FI
>T51:/FI
>O51:@IF(@SUM(E51-F51+G51-H51+I51-J51)=@SUM(K51-L51+M51-N51),@TRUE,@FALSE)
>N51:/F$
>M51:/F$
>L51:/F$
>K51:/F$@IF(E51-F51+G51-H51+I51-J51>0,E51-F51+G51-H51+I51-J51,0)
>J51:/F$
>I51:/F$
>H51:/F$
>G51:/F$
>F51:/F$
>E51:/F$
>B51:"RATES
>A51:/FL+A50+1
>U50:/FI
>T50:/FI
>O50:@IF(@SUM(E50-F50+G50-H50+I50-J50)=@SUM(K50-L50+M50-N50),@TRUE,@FALSE)
>N50:/F$
>M50:/F$
>L50:/F$
>K50:/F$@IF(E50-F50+G50-H50+I50-J50>0,E50-F50+G50-H50+I50-J50,0)
>J50:/F$
>I50:/F$
>H50:/F$
>G50:/F$
>F50:/F$
>E50:/F$
>B50:"RENT
>A50:/FL+A49+1
>U49:/FI
>T49:/FI
>O49:@IF(@SUM(E49-F49+G49-H49+I49-J49)=@SUM(K49-L49+M49-N49),@TRUE,@FALSE)
>N49:/F$
>M49:/F$
>L49:/F$
>K49:/F$@IF(E49-F49+G49-H49+I49-J49>0,E49-F49+G49-H49+I49-J49,0)
>J49:/F$
>I49:/F$
>H49:/F$
>G49:/F$
>F49:/F$
>E49:/F$
>C49:"ENT
>B49:"RECRUITM
>A49:/FL+A48+1
>U48:/FI
>T48:/FI+T15-T45
>S48:/-.
>R48:"/PROFIT................
>Q48:"NET LOSS/PROFIT................
```

```
>O48:@IF(@SUM(E48-F48+G48-H48+I48-J48)=@SUM(K48-L48+M48-N48),@TRUE,@FALSE)
>N48:/F$
>M48:/F$
>L48:/F$
>K48:/F$@IF(E48-F48+G48-H48+I48-J48>0,E48-F48+G48-H48+I48-J48,0)
>J48:/F$
>I48:/F$
>H48:/F$
>G48:/F$
>F48:/F$
>E48:/F$
>D48:"RATION
>C48:"S REMUNE
>B48:"DIRECTOR
>A48:/FL+A47+1
>U47:/FI
>T47:/FI
>O47:@IF(@SUM(E47-F47+G47-H47+I47-J47)=@SUM(K47-L47+M47-N47),@TRUE,@FALSE)
>N47:/F$
>M47:/F$
>L47:/F$
>K47:/F$@IF(E47-F47+G47-H47+I47-J47>0,E47-F47+G47-H47+I47-J47,0)
>J47:/F$
>I47:/F$
>H47:/F$
>G47:/F$
>F47:/F$
>E47:/F$
>D47:"IVE
>C47:" PRODUCT
>B47:"SALARIES
>A47:/FL+A46+1
>U46:/FI
>T46:/FI
>O46:@IF(@SUM(E46-F46+G46-H46+I46-J46)=@SUM(K46-L46+M46-N46),@TRUE,@FALSE)
>N46:/F$
>M46:/F$
>L46:/F$
>K46:/F$@IF(E46-F46+G46-H46+I46-J46>0,E46-F46+G46-H46+I46-J46,0)
>J46:/F$
>I46:/F$
>H46:/F$
>G46:/F$
>F46:/F$
>E46:/F$
>C46:" ADMIN
>B46:"SALARIES
>A46:/FL+A45+1
>U45:/FI
>T45:/FI@SUM(T18...T44)
>O45:@IF(@SUM(E45-F45+G45-H45+I45-J45)=@SUM(K45-L45+M45-N45),@TRUE,@FALSE)
>N45:/F$
>M45:/F$
>L45:/F$
>K45:/F$@IF(E45-F45+G45-H45+I45-J45>0,E45-F45+G45-H45+I45-J45,0)
>J45:/F$
>I45:/F$
>H45:/F$
>G45:/F$
>F45:/F$
>E45:/F$
```

```
)C45:"NTRACT
)B45:"SUB - CO
)A45:/FL+A44+1
)U44:/FI
)T44:/FI/-
)O44:@IF(@SUM(E44-F44+G44-H44+I44-J44)=@SUM(K44-L44+M44-N44),@TRUE,@FALSE)
)N44:/F$
)M44:/F$
)L44:/F$
)K44:/F$@IF(E44-F44+G44-H44+I44-J44)0,E44-F44+G44-H44+I44-J44,0)
)J44:/F$
)I44:/F$
)H44:/F$
)G44:/F$
)F44:/F$
)E44:/F$
)C44:"NCY FEES
)B44:"CONSULTA
)A44:/FL601
)U43:/FI
)T43:/FI
)O43:@IF(@SUM(E43-F43+G43-H43+I43-J43)=@SUM(K43-L43+M43-N43),@TRUE,@FALSE)
)N43:/F$
)M43:/F$
)L43:/F$
)K43:/F$
)J43:/F$
)I43:/F$
)H43:/F$
)G43:/F$
)F43:/F$
)E43:/F$
)A43:/FL
)U42:/FI
)T42:/FI
)O42:@IF(@SUM(E42-F42+G42-H42+I42-J42)=@SUM(K42-L42+M42-N42),@TRUE,@FALSE)
)N42:/F$
)M42:/F$
)L42:/F$@IF(E42-F42+G42-H42+I42-J42)<0,-1*(E42-F42+G42-H42+I42-J42),0)
)K42:/F$
)J42:/F$
)I42:/F$
)H42:/F$
)G42:/F$
)F42:/F$
)E42:/F$
)C42:"OTHER
)B42:"SALES -
)A42:/FL+A41+1
)Y41:-2548
)U41:/FI
)T41:/FI+K94
)S41:"ST
)R41:"N INTERE
)Q41:"BANK LOA
)O41:@IF(@SUM(E41-F41+G41-H41+I41-J41)=@SUM(K41-L41+M41-N41),@TRUE,@FALSE)
)N41:/F$
)M41:/F$
)L41:/F$@IF(E41-F41+G41-H41+I41-J41)<0,-1*(E41-F41+G41-H41+I41-J41),0)
)K41:/F$
```

```
>J41:/F$
>I41:/F$
>H41:/F$
>G41:/F$
>F41:/F$
>E41:/F$
>C41:"TYPE 5
>B41:"SALES -
>A41:/FL+A40+1
>U40:/FI
>T40:/FI+K91
>S40:"NTEREST
>R40:"rges & I
>Q40:"Bank Cha
>O40:@IF(@SUM(E40-F40+G40-H40+I40-J40)=@SUM(K40-L40+M40-N40),@TRUE,@FALSE)
>N40:/F$
>M40:/F$
>L40:/F$@IF(E40-F40+G40-H40+I40-J40)<0,-1*(E40-F40+G40-H40+I40-J40),0)
>K40:/F$
>J40:/F$
>I40:/F$
>H40:/F$
>G40:/F$
>F40:/F$
>E40:/F$
>C40:"TYPE 4
>B40:"SALES -
>A40:/FL+A39+1
>U39:/FI
>T39:/FI+K90
>R39:"est
>Q39:"HP Inter
>O39:@IF(@SUM(E39-F39+G39-H39+I39-J39)=@SUM(K39-L39+M39-N39),@TRUE,@FALSE)
>N39:/F$
>M39:/F$
>L39:/F$@IF(E39-F39+G39-H39+I39-J39)<0,-1*(E39-F39+G39-H39+I39-J39),0)
>K39:/F$
>J39:/F$
>I39:/F$
>H39:/F$
>G39:/F$
>F39:/F$
>E39:/F$
>C39:"TYPE 3
>B39:"SALES -
>A39:/FL+A38+1
>U38:/FI
>T38:/FI+K92+K93
>R38:"TION
>Q38:"DEPRECIA
>O38:@IF(@SUM(E38-F38+G38-H38+I38-J38)=@SUM(K38-L38+M38-N38),@TRUE,@FALSE)
>N38:/F$
>M38:/F$
>L38:/F$@IF(E38-F38+G38-H38+I38-J38)<0,-1*(E38-F38+G38-H38+I38-J38),0)
>K38:/F$
>J38:/F$
>I38:/F$
>H38:/F$
>G38:/F$
>F38:/F$
```

```
>E38:/F$
>C38:"TYPE 2
>B38:"SALES -
>A38:/FL+A37+1
>U37:/FI
>T37:/FI@SUM(K101...K104)
>R37:"ES
>Q37:"INSURANC
>O37:@IF(@SUM(E37-F37+G37-H37+I37-J37)=@SUM(K37-L37+M37-N37),@TRUE,@FALSE)
>N37:/F$>M37:/F$
>L37:/F$@IF(E37-F37+G37-H37+I37-J37)<0,-1*(E37-F37+G37-H37+I37-J37),0)
>K37:/F$
>J37:/F$
>I37:/F$
>H37:/F$
>G37:/F$
>F37:/F$
>E37:/F$
>C37:"TYPE 1
>B37:"SALES -
>A37:/FL501
>U36:/FI
>T36:/FI+K96
>Q36:"SUNDRY
>O36:@IF(@SUM(E36-F36+G36-H36+I36-J36)=@SUM(K36-L36+M36-N36),@TRUE,@FALSE)
>N36:/F$
>M36:/F$
>L36:/F$
>K36:/F$
>J36:/F$
>I36:/F$
>H36:/F$
>G36:/F$
>F36:/F$
>E36:/F$
>A36:/FL
>U35:/FI
>T35:/FI+K76
>S35:"EXHIBS
>R35:"ING AND
>Q35:"ADVERTIS
>O35:@IF(@SUM(E35-F35+G35-H35+I35-J35)=@SUM(K35-L35+M35-N35),@TRUE,@FALSE)
>N35:/F$@IF(E35-F35+G35-H35+I35-J35)<0,-1*(E35-F35+G35-H35+I35-J35),0)
>M35:/F$@IF(E35-F35+G35-H35+I35-J35)0,E35-F35+G35-H35+I35-J35,0)
>L35:/F$
>K35:/F$
>J35:/F$
>I35:/F$
>H35:/F$
>G35:/F$
>F35:/F$
>E35:/F$
>C35:"N
>B35:"BANK LOA
>A35:/FL+A34+1
>U34:/FI
>T34:/FI+K79
>S34:"VATIONS
>R34:"AND RENO
>Q34:"REPAIRS
```

```
>O34:@IF(@SUM(E34-F34+G34-H34+I34-J34)=@SUM(K34-L34+M34-N34),@TRUE,@FALSE)
>N34:/F$@IF(E34-F34+G34-H34+I34-J34)<0,-1*(E34-F34+G34-H34+I34-J34),0)
>M34:/F$@IF(E34-F34+G34-H34+I34-J34>0,E34-F34+G34-H34+I34-J34,0)
>L34:/F$
>K34:/F$
>J34:/F$
>I34:/F$
>H34:/F$
>G34:/F$
>F34:/F$
>E34:/F$
>D34:"ENCE
>C34:"EST SUSP
>B34:"HP INTER
>A34:/FL+A33+1
>U33:/FI
>T33:/FI+K88
>R33:"ES
>Q33:"LEGAL FE
>O33:@IF(@SUM(E33-F33+G33-H33+I33-J33)=@SUM(K33-L33+M33-N33),@TRUE,@FALSE)
>N33:/F$@IF(E33-F33+G33-H33+I33-J33)<0,-1*(E33-F33+G33-H33+I33-J33),0)
>M33:/F$@IF(E33-F33+G33-H33+I33-J33>0,E33-F33+G33-H33+I33-J33,0)
>L33:/F$
>K33:/F$
>J33:/F$
>I33:/F$
>H33:/F$
>G33:/F$
>F33:/F$
>E33:/F$
>B33:"RESERVES
>A33:/FL+A32+1
>U32:/FI
>T32:/FI+K87
>S32:"TANCY
>R32:"d ACCOUN
>Q32:"AUDIT AN
>O32:@IF(@SUM(E32-F32+G32-H32+I32-J32)=@SUM(K32-L32+M32-N32),@TRUE,@FALSE)
>N32:/F$@IF(E32-F32+G32-H32+I32-J32)<0,-1*(E32-F32+G32-H32+I32-J32),0)
>M32:/F$@IF(E32-F32+G32-H32+I32-J32>0,E32-F32+G32-H32+I32-J32,0)
>L32:/F$
>K32:/F$
>J32:/F$
>I32:/F$
>H32:/F$
>G32:/F$
>F32:/F$
>E32:/F$
>C32:"PITAL
>B32:"SHARE CA
>A32:/FL401
>U31:/F
>T31:/FI+K97+K98
>S31:"S ETC
>R31:"BS.PAPER
>Q31:"BOOOK.SU
>O31:@IF(@SUM(E31-F31+G31-H31+I31-J31)=@SUM(K31-L31+M31-N31),@TRUE,@FALSE)
>N31:/F$
>M31:/F$
>L31:/F$
```

```
>K31:/F$
>J31:/F$
>I31:/F$
>H31:/F$
>G31:/F$
>F31:/F$
>E31:/F$
>A31:/FL
>U30:/FI
>T30:/FI+K77+K78
>S30:")
>R30:"S
>Q30:"COMPUTER
>O30:@IF(@SUM(E30-F30+G30-H30+I30-J30)=@SUM(K30-L30+M30-N30),@TRUE,@FALSE)
>N30:/F$
>M30:/F$
>L30:/F$
>K30:/F$
>J30:/F$
>I30:/F$
>H30:/F$
>G30:/F$
>F30:/F$
>E30:/F$
>A30:/FL
>U29:/FI
>T29:/FI
>S29:")
>R29:"IER
>Q29:"PHOTOCOP
>O29:@IF(@SUM(E29-F29+G29-H29+I29-J29)=@SUM(K29-L29+M29-N29),@TRUE,@FALSE)
>N29:/F$
>M29:/F$
>L29:/F$
>K29:/F$
>J29:/F$
>I29:/F$
>H29:/F$
>G29:/F$
>F29:/F$
>E29:/F$
>A29:/FL
>U28:/FI
>T28:/FI+K54+K55
>S28:"D STAT.
>R28:" POST AN
>Q28:"PRINTING,
>O28:@IF(@SUM(E28-F28+G28-H28+I28-J28)=@SUM(K28-L28+M28-N28),@TRUE,@FALSE)
>N28:/F$
>M28:/F$
>L28:/F$
>K28:/F$
>J28:/F$
>I28:/F$
>H28:/F$
>G28:/F$
>F28:/F$
>E28:/F$
>C28:"PROGRESS
>B28:"WORK IN
```

```
>A28:/FL+A27+1
>U27:/FI
>T27:/FI+K89
>Q27:"LEASING
>027:@IF(@SUM(E27-F27+G27-H27+I27-J27)=@SUM(K27-L27+M27-N27),@TRUE,@FALSE)
>N27:/F$@IF(E27-F27+G27-H27+I27-J27)<0,-1*(E27-F27+G27-H27+I27-J27),0)
>M27:/F$@IF(E27-F27+G27-H27+I27-J27)>0,E27-F27+G27-H27+I27-J27,0)
>L27:/F$
>K27:/F$
>J27:/F$
>I27:/F$
>H27:/F$
>G27:/F$
>F27:/F$
>E27:/F$
>B27:"HP CAR 2
>A27:/FL+A26+1
>U26:/FI
>T6:/FI+K83
>S26:"ACCOM.
>R26:"NCE AND
>Q26:"SUBSISTA
>026:@IF(@SUM(E26-F26+G26-H26+I26-J26)=@SUM(K26-L26+M26-N26),@TRUE,@FALSE)
>N26:/F$@IF(E26-F26+G26-H26+I26-J26)<0,-1*(E26-F26+G26-H26+I26-J26),0)
>M26:/F$@IF(E26-F26+G26-H26+I26-J26)>0,E26-F26+G26-H26+I26-J26,0)
>L26:/F$
>K26:/F$
>J26:/F$
>I26:/F$
>H26:/F$
>G26:/F$
>F26:/F$
>E26:/F$
>B26:"HP CAR 1
>A26:/FL+A25+1
>U25:/FI
>T25:/FI@SUM(K81...K82,K84...K85)
>S25:"INMENT
>R25:" ENTERTA
>Q25:"TRAVEL &
>025:@IF(@SUM(E25-F25+G25-H25+I25-J25)=@SUM(K25-L25+M25-N25),@TRUE,@FALSE)
>N25:/F$
>M25:/F$
>L25:/F$
>K25:/F$
>J25:/F$
>I25:/F$
>H25:/F$
>G25:/F$
>F25:/F$
>E25:/F$
>B25:"NET PAY
>A25:/FL+A24+1
>U24:/FI
>T24:/FI+K80
>R24:"PENSES
>Q24:"MOTOR EX
>024:@IF(@SUM(E24-F24+G24-H24+I24-J24)=@SUM(K24-L24+M24-N24),@TRUE,@FALSE)
>N24:/F$
>M24:/F$
```

```
>L24:/F$
>K24:/F$
>J24:/F$@IF(+E24-F24)<0,-1*(+E24-F24),+E24-F24)
>I24:/F$
>H24:/F$
>G24:/F$
>F24:/F$
>E24:/F$
>C24:".I.C.
>B24:"PAYE - N
>A24:/FL+A23+1
>U23:/FI
>T23:/FI+K53
>S23:"LEX
>R23:"E AND TE
>Q23:"TELEPHON
>O23:@IF(@SUM(E23-F23+G23-H23+I23-J23)=@SUM(K23-L23+M23-N23),@TRUE,@FALSE)
>N23:/F$
>M23:/F$
>L23:/F$
>K23:/F$
>J23:/F$@IF(+E23-F23)<0,-1*(+E23-F23),+E23-F23)
>I23:/F$
>H23:/F$
>G23:/F$
>F23:/F$
>E23:/F$
>B23:"V.A.T.
>A23:/FL+A22+1
>U22:/FI
>T22:/FI+K50+K51+K52
>S22:"SERVICES
>R22:"TES AND
>Q22:"RENT, RA
>O22:@IF(@SUM(E22-F22+G22-H22+I22-J22)=@SUM(K22-L22+M22-N22),@TRUE,@FALSE)
>N22:/F$
>M22:/F$
>L22:/F$
>K22:/F$
>J22:/F$@IF(+E22-F22)<0,-1*(+E22-F22),+E22-F22)
>I22:/F$
>H22:/F$
>G22:/F$
>F22:/F$
>E22:/F$
>C22:"DGER
>B22:"SALESLE>R21:"ENT
>A22:/FL+A21+1>Q21:"RECRUITM
>U21:/FI
>T21:/FI+K49
>O21:@IF(@SUM(E21-F21+G21-H21+I21-J21)=@SUM(K21-L21+M21-N21),@TRUE,@FALSE)
>N21:/F$
>M21:/F$
>L21:/F$
>K21:/F$
>J21:/F$
>I21:/F$@IF(+E21-F21)<0,-1*(+E21-F21),+E21-F21)
>H21:/F$
>G21:/F$
>F21:/F$
>E21:/F$
```

```
>C21:"EDGER
>B21:"BOUGHT L
>A21:/FL301
>U20:/FI
>T20:/FI+K45+K44
>R20:"RACT
>Q20:"SUB-CONT
>O20:@IF(@SUM(E20-F20+G20-H20+I20-J20)=@SUM(K20-L20+M20-N20),@TRUE,@FALSE)
>N20:/F$
>M20:/F$
>L20:/F$
>K20:/F$
>J20:/F$
>I20:/F$
>H20:/F$
>G20:/F$
>F20:/F$
>E20:/F$
>A20:/FL
>U19:/FI
>T19:/FI+K46+K47
>Q19:"SALARIES
>O19:@IF(@SUM(E19-F19+G19-H19-I19-J19)=@SUM(K19-L19+M19-N19),@TRUE,@FALSE)
>N19:/F$@IF(E19-F19+G19-H19+I19-J19)<0,-1*(E19-F19+G19-H19+I19-J19),0)
>M19:/F$@IF(E19-F19+G19-H19+I19-J19)0,E19-F19+G19-H19+I19-J19,0)
>L19:/F$
>K19:/F$
>J19:/F$
>I19:/F$
>H19:/F$
>G19:/F$
>F19:/F$
>E19:/F$
>C19:"HAND
>B19:"CASH IN
>A19:/FL+A18+1
>U18:/FI
>T18:/FI+K48
>S18:"RATION
>R18:"S REMUNE
>Q18:"DIRECTOR'
>O18:@IF(@SUM(E18-F18+G18-H18+I18-J18)=@SUM(K18-L18+M18-N18),@TRUE,@FALSE)
>N18:/F$@IF(E18-F18+G18-H18+I18-J18)<0,-1*(E18-F18+G18-H18+I18-J18),0)
>M18:/F$@IF(E18-F18+G18-H18+I18-J18)0,E18-F18+G18-H18+I18-J18,0)
>L18:/F$
>K18:/F$
>J18:/F$
>I18:/F$
>H18:/F$
>G18:/F$
>F18:/F$
>E18:/F$
>C18:" SOCIETY
>B18:"BUILDING
>A18:/FL+A17+1
>U17:/FI
>T17:/FI
>R17:"-
>Q17:"——
>O17:@IF(@SUM(E17-F17+G17-H17+I17-J17)=@SUM(K17-L17+M17-N17),@TRUE,@FALSE)
>N17:/F$@IF(E17-F17+G17-H17+I17-J17)<0,-1*(E17-F17+G17-H17+I17-J17),0)
>M16:/F$@IF(E17-F17+G17-H17+I17-J17)0,E17-F17+G17-H17+I17-J17,0)
```

```
>L17:/F$
>K17:/F$
>J17:/F$
>I17:/F$
>H17:/F$
>G17:/F$
>F17:/F$
>E17:/F$
>D17:" 2
>C17:"OUNT NO.
>B17:"BANK ACC
>A17:/FL+A16+1
>U16:/FI
>T16:/FI
>R16:"S
>Q16:"OVERHEAD
>O16:@IF(@SUM(E16-F16+G16-H16+I16-J16)=@SUM(K16-L16+M16-N16),@TRUE,@FALSE)
>N16:/F$@IF(E16-F16+G16-H16+I16-J16)<0,-1*(E16-F16+G16-H16+I16-J16),0)
>M16:/F$@IF(E16-F16+G16-H16+I16-J16)>0,E16-F16+G16-H16+I16-J16,0)
>K16:/F$
>J16:/F$
>I16:/F$
>H16:/F$
>F16:/F$
>E16:/F$
>D16:" 1
>C16:"OUNT NO.
>A16:/FL201
>U15:/FI
>T15:/FI+T10+T12-T11
>O15:@IF(@SUM(E15-F15+G15-H15+I15-J15)=@SUM(K15-L15+M15-N15),@TRUE,@FALSE)
>N15:/F$@IF(E15-F15+G15-H15+I15-J15)<0,-1*(E15-F15+G15-H15+I15-J15),0)
>M15:/F$@IF(E15-F15+G15-H15+I15-J15)>0,E15-F15+G15-H15+I15-J15,0)
>L15:/F$
>K15:/F$
>J15:/F$
>I15:/F$
>H15:/F$
>G15:/F$
>F15:/F$
>E15:/F$
>A15:/FL
>U14:/FI
>T14:/FI"-------
>O14:@IF(@SUM(E14-F14+G14-H14+I14-J14)=@SUM(K14-L14+M14-N14),@TRUE,@FALSE)
>N14:/F$@IF(E14-F14+G14-H14+I14-J14)<0,-1*(E14-F14+G14-H14+I14-J14),0)
>M14:/F$@IF(E14-F14+G14-H14+I14-J14)>0,E14-F14+G14-H14+I14-J14,0)
>L14:/F$
>K14:/F$
>J14:/F$
>I14:/F$
>H14:/F$
>G14:/F$
>F14:/F$
>E14:/F$
>C14:"TION
>B14:"DEPRECIA
>A14:/FL+A13+1
>U13:/FI
>T13:/FI
>O13:@IF(@SUM(E13-F13+G13-H13+I13-J13)=@SUM(K13-L13+M13-N13),@TRUE,@FALSE)
>N13:/F$@IF(E13-F13+G13-H13+I13-J13)<0,-1*(E13-F13+G13-H13+I13-J13),0)
>M13:/F$@IF(E13-F13+G13-H13+I13-J13)>0,E13-F13+G13-H13+I13-J13,0)
```

```
>L13:/F$
>K13:/F$
>J13:/F$
>I13:/F$
>H13:/F$
>G13:/F$
>F13:/F$
>E13:/F$
>C13:"TION
>B13:"DEPRECIA
>A13:/FL+A12+1
>U12:/FI
>T12:/FI+L28
>R12:"WIP
>Q12:"CLOSING
>O12:@IF(@SUM(E12-F12+G12-H12+I12-J12)=@SUM(K12-L12+M12-N12),@TRUE,@FALSE)
>N12:/F$@IF(E12-F12+G12-H12+I12-J12)<0,-1*(E12-F12+G12-H12+I12-J12),0)
>M12:/F$@IF(E12-F12+G12-H12+I12-J12)>0,E12-F12+G12-H12+I12-J12,0)
>L12:/F$
>K12:/F$
>J12:/F$
>I12:/F$
>H12:/F$
>G12:/F$
>F12:/F$
>E12:/F$
>C12:"ST
>B12:"OFF&F CO
>A12:/FL+A11+1
>U11:/FI
>T11:/FI+K28
>S11:"G WIP
>R11:"D OPENIN
>Q11:"STOCK AN
>O11:@IF(@SUM(E11-F11+G11-H11+I11-J11)=@SUM(K11-L11+M11-N11),@TRUE,@FALSE)
>N11:/F$@IF(E11-F11+G11-H11+I11-J11)<0,-1*(E11-F11+G11-H11+I11-J11),0)
>M11:/F$@IF(E11-F11+G11-H11+I11-J11)>0,E11-F11+G11-H11+I11-J11,0)
>L11:/F$
>K11:/F$
>J11:/F$
>I11:/F$
>H11:/F$
>G11:/F$
>F11:/F$
>E11:/F$
>D11:"OST
>C11:"HICLES C
>B11:"MOTOR VE
>A11:/FL101
>U10:/FI
>T10:/FI@SUM(L37...L42)
>Q10:"SALES
>N10:"    -
>M10:"    +
>L10:"    -
>K10:"    +
>J10:"    -
>I10:"    +
>H10:"    -
>G10:"    +
>F10:"    -
>E10:"    +
>A10:/FL
>N9:/FR"    CR
>M9:/FR"    DR
>L9:/FR"    CR
>K9:/FR"    DR
>J9:/FR"    CR
>I9:/FR"    DR
>H9:/FR"    CR
>G9:/FR"    DR
>F9:/FR"    CR
>E9:/FR"    DR
>A9:/FL
>T8:/-
>N8:/-
>M8:/-
>L8:/-
>K8:/-
>J8:/-
>I8:/-
>H8:/-
>G8:/-
>F8:/-
>E8:/-
>D8:/-
>C8:/-
>B8:/-
>A8:/-
>T7:/FR"TO DATE
>J7:/FR"PAYMENTS
>B7:"E
>A7:"REFERENCE
>T6:/FR"YEAR
>N6:/FR"SHEET
>L6:"  & LOSS
>K6:"=
>J6:/FR"& PRE-
>I6:/FR"ACCRUALS
>H6:/FR
>F6:"NCES
>E6:/FR"BALA
>A6:/FL"N/LEDGER
>T5:/FR
>N5:/FL"ANCE
>M5:/FR"BAL
>L5:/FL"FIT
>K5:/FR"PRO
>J5:/FR"DEBTORS
>I5:/FR"ITORS &
>H5:/FL"TMENTS
>G5:/FR"ADJUS
>F5:/FL"L
>E5:/FR"N/
>C5:"PTION
>B5:"  DESCRI
>U4:/FR/-=
>T4:/FR"=
>I4:/FR"CRED-
>U3:"NAUDITED
>T3:/FR"U
>H3:/-
>G3:/-
>F3:/-
```

```
)D3:"======
)C3:/-=
)B3:"=====================
)U2:"—
)T2:/—
)S2:/—
)R2:/—
)Q2:/—
)H2:/FR"YEAR
)G2:"- MONTH
)F2:/FR"MONTH
)D2:"ALANCE
)C2:" TRIAL B
)B2:"EXTENDED
)U1:"UNT
)T1:"OSS ACCO
)S1:"IT AND L
)R1:"AND PROF
)Q1:"TRADING
/W1
/GOC
/GRM
/GF$
/GC8
/X!/X
)A1:
```

19

Educational templates

This chapter is lamentably short! All we can do is to give you a couple of examples; the rest is up to your imagination and requirements.

Examples of two types of templates are given. The first helps with administration and the second could be used as a teaching aid. The use of logical operators (@NOT, @AND, @OR) can be a powerful aid in helping to pick and choose various criteria. For example:-

```
@IF(@AND(B14>10,C14<50),5,0)
```

(see cell F14 'Teacher Admin. Template') selects those pupils who are over the age of 10 AND whose marks are less than 50. Other selection criteria can be substituted. Instead of using the * format to flag those pupils who meet the criteria, actual figures could be displayed instead.

The moments-about-a-point template shows how a relatively primitive visual aid can be constructed. It may generate a few useful ideas!

```
          A          B          C          D          E          F          G
     ___________________________________________________________________
  1  EXAMPLE OF TEACHER ADMIN TEMPLATE
  2  __________________________________
  3
  4                                                            AGE OVER
  5                                                             10 AND
  6  NAME               AGE      MARKS    PASSES     FAILURES       FAIL
  7  ___________________________________________________________________
  8  JOHN                10        45                *****
  9  MICHAEL             11        82     *****
 10  DON                 10        63     *****
 11  MARIAN              10        74     *****
 12  MARTHA              11        32                *****         *****
 13  TOMMY               10        51     *****
 14  SARAH                9        50     ******
 15
 16
 17
 18                     AGE     MARK
 19
 20  AVERAGES            10        45
```

```
>A29:/FL
>A28:/FL
>A27:/FL
>A26:/FL
>A25:/FL
>A24:/FL
>A23:/FL
>A22:/FL
>A21:/FL
>C20:/FI@AVERAGE(C8...C4
>B20:/FI@AVERAGE(B8...B14
>A20:/FL''AVERAGES
>A19:/FL
>C18:/FR''MARK
>B18:/FR''AGE
>A18:/FL
>A17:/FL
>A16:/FL
>A15:/FL
>F14:/F*@IF(@AND(B14>10,C14<50),5,0
>E14:/F*@IF(@NOT(C14>=50),5,0)
>D14:/F*@IF(C14>=50,5,0)
>C14:/FI50
>B14:/FI9
>A14:/FL''SARAH
>F13:/F*@IF(@AND(B13>10,C13<50),5,0
>E13:/F*@IF(@NOT(C13>=50),5,0)
>D13:/F*@IF(C13>=50,5,0)
>C13:/FR51
>B13:/FR10
>A13:/FL''TOMMY
>F12:/F*@IF(@AND(B12>10,C12<50),5,0
>E12:/F*@IF(@NOT(C12>=50),5,0)
>D12:/F*@IF(C12>=50,5,0)
>C12:/FR32
>B12:/FR11
>A12:/FL''MARTHA
>F11:/F*@IF(@AND(B11>10,C11<50),5,0
>E11:/F*@IF(@NOT(C11>=50),5,0)
>D11:/F*@IF(C11>=50,5,0)
>C11:/FR74
>B11:/FR10
>A11:/FL''MARIAN
>F10:/F*@IF(@AND(B10>10,C10<50),5,0
>E10:/F*@IF(@NOT(C10>=50),5,0)
>D10:/F*@IF(C10>=50,5,0)
>C10:/FR63
>B10:/FR10
>A10:/FL''DON
>F9:/F*@IF(@AND(B9>10,C9<50),5,0
>E9:/F*@IF(@NOT(C9>=50),5,0)
>D9:/F*@IF(C9>=50,5,0)
>C9:/FR82
>B9:/FR11
>A9:/FL''MICHAEL
>F8:/F*@IF(@AND(B8>10,C8<50),5,0
>E8:/F*@IF(@NOT(C8>=50),5,0)
>D8:/F*@IF(C8>=50,5,0)
>C8:/FR45
>B8:/FR10
>A8:/FL''JOHN
>G7:/-
>F7:/-
>E7:/-
>D7:/-
>C7:/-
>B7:/-
>A7:/-
>F6:/FR''FAIL
>E6:/FR''FAILURES
>D6:/FR''PASSES
>C6:/FR''MARKS
>B6:/FR''AGE
>A6:/FL''NAME
>F5:/FR''10 AND
>D5:/FR
>F4:''AGE OVER
>D3:/FR
>D2:/-
>C2:/-
>B2:/-
>A2:/-
>D1:''MPLATE
>C1:'' ADMIN TEMP
>B1:''F TEACHER
>A1:''EXAMPLE OF
/W1
/GOC
/GRA
/GFL
/GC9
/X-/X>A1:>A1:
```

```
    MOMENTS ABOUT A POINT

   D     F2       D2
<------->!<-------------->
          V
--------------------------
↑                        ↑
PIVOT                    F3


                         4.05

FORCE F2 DIST. D1 DIST. D2
-------------------------
     10       8.5     12.5
-------------------------
```

```
>C20:/—
>B20:/—
>A20:/—
>C19:12.5
>B19:8.5
>A19:10
>C18:/—
>B18:/—
>A18:/—
>C17:/FR''DIST. D2
>B17:/FR''DIST. D1
>A17:/FR''FORCE F2
>D14:/F$+A19*B19/(B19+C19)
>D12:''  F3
>A12:''  PIVOT
>D11:''  ↑
>A11:''  ↑
>D10:''—
>C10:/—
>B10:/—
>A10:''  ——
>B9:''    V
>D8:''→
>C8:''——
>B8:''→!←
>A8:''    ←
>C7:''   D2
>B7:''    F2
>A7:''      D1
>C5:'' A POINT
>B5:''NTS ABOUT
>A5:''     MOME
/W1
/GOC
/GRA
/GC9
/X!/X>A1:>A19:
```

20

Production planning

One of the tedious calculation jobs performed by the production planning department in most manufacturing concerns is that of trying to perform the impossible task of balancing the demands of the sales department for instant delivery of every order with the production departments' desire for an even workload and the accountant's desire to keep overtime payments to a minimum. Coupled with these is the Managing Director's demand to know whether Production can meet that impossible delivery date and ridiculously low price he's just negotiated on the golf course! Enough to make the production control manager tear his hair and threaten to resign once again? Not with VisiCalc! It's easy to set up a table which will add up the hours required of each manufacturing facility and give both weekly and monthly capacity summaries. However, the clever part lies in being able to juggle orders in order to find the work pattern which best keeps sales, production and accounts happy. The MOVE (/MR) command can move complete rows around the worksheet so that orders can be shuffled around and the capacity requirements recalculated as required. The following example illustrates this:

	A	B	C	D	E	F	G
1		DOUBLE GLAZING CO. PRODUCTION PLAN (MAN-HRS)					
2							
3		ORDER	CUT	CUT	ASSEMBLE	ASSEMBLE	SHIP &
4	WEEK NO.	REF	GLASS	FRAMING	FRAME	+ GLASS	INSTALL
5							
6		MCTAVISH	34	48	23	14	8
7		JONES &CO	170	265	55	35	40
8							
9							
10		REQ. B/F					
11	1	CAPY REQD	204	313	78	49	48
12		AVAILABLE	200	300	150	100	125
13		UNUSED	0	0	72	51	77
14		OVERLOAD	4	13	0	0	0
15							
16		BROWN CO.	70	232	96	56	30
17		ROLLER CO	350	563	274	96	54
18		CARTER	25	35	15	10	5
19							
20							
21		REQ. B/F	4	13	0	0	0
22	2	CAPY REQD	449	843	385	162	89
23		AVAILABLE	200	300	150	100	25
24		UNUSED	0	0	0	0	36
25		OVERLOAD	249	543	235	62	0
26							
27		GLASS CO.	35	25	40	15	25
28							
29							
30		REQ. B/F	249	543	235	62	0
31	3	CAPY REQD	284	568	275	77	25
32		AVAILABLE	200	300	150	100	250
33		UNUSED	0	0	0	23	35
34		OVERLOAD	84	268	125	0	0
35							
36							
37							
38							
39		REQ. B/F	84	268	125	0	0
40	4	CAPY REQD	84	268	125	0	0
41		AVAILABLE	200	300	150	100	250
42		UNUSED	116	32	25	100	250
43		OVERLOAD	0	0	0	0	0
44							
45							
46							
47							
48	MONTH	CAPY REQD	684	1168	503	226	162
49		AVAILABLE	800	1200	600	400	750
50		UNUSED	116	32	97	174	588
51		OVERLOAD	0	0	0	0	0
52							
53							

For any particular week, the capacity required (CAPY REQD) row is the sum of ALL the rows above it up to (and including) the first double underline row (===) above it. Thus it is the sum of the man-hours required for each order in a particular week plus the overload from the previous week. Since the range to be summed includes two dotted lines, any row inserted between these dotted lines will be included in the calculations automatically. For example, cell C22 will contain the formula @SUM(C15...C21). The dotted lines have arithmetic values of zero, so can be included in most formulae without causing problems.

To insert a fresh order, place the cursor just below the double dotted line at the top of the appropriate week and type /IR. Now type in the order details (and press ! if necessary to recalculate the sheet). If any particular week shows an overload, try moving an order from that week to some other week. To do this, place the cursor on the row containing the order to be moved and type /MR. Now press the dot key (an ellipsis will be supplied by VisiCalc instead of the dot), move the cursor to the row above which you wish the order to be inserted, and press 'return'. Now recalculate the sheet if required. Examine the capacity figures and move another order if necessary. When you're happy (or have done the best production load smoothing possible in the circumstances), print the resulting planning sheet.

The only slightly less than straight forward formulae used are those which calculate the 'unused' and 'overload' figures.
The first is calculated using the algorithm

> If 'available' is greater than 'capy reqd'
> then use 'available' minus 'capy reqd'
> otherwise, use zero.

The second uses a very similar algorithm

> If 'available' is less than 'capy reqd'
> then use 'capy reqd' minus 'available'
> otherwise, use zero.

An improvement could be to enter the weekly capacity available figures only once at the top of the sheet (perhaps in week 1) and use very simple formulae to transfer these figures to the other weeks. For example, week 1 available capacity figures are in cells C12 to G12 and can be copied to week 2 merely by inserting the formula +C12 in cell C23, +D12 in cell D23 and so on. Thus, any changes made to row 12 will be reflected automatically in row 23 and so on. If any particular available capacity cell must contain some different figure, perhaps because of staff illness or holiday, then the new figure is merely typed into the correct cell. Of course, this will destroy the formula that was already in that cell. Any number already appearing in the planning sheet as the result of a calculation can be "frozen" by placing the cursor on that cell and typing #. This is equivalent to destroying the formula in that cell by typing a value into it.

A complete listing of the template used in the above example is not included here since only the principle is common to many manufacturing concerns, not the details. In any case, there's nothing complicated about the calculations involved.

Machine Scheduling

The situation frequently arises in manufacturing where a range of products can each be made on a number of different machines. For each item there is a preferred machine but many items can be made on alternative machines but at the penalty of longer manufacturing times. Since orders are usually received spread over a period, it is not unusual to load the machines as the orders are received, using the "preferred" machines if capacity is available or "second preference" machines if it is not. Eventually, there will arise a need to perform considerable schedule juggling to even out the loads on the various machines. Normally this is performed by inspecting the schedule and swapping jobs amongst the machines and this involves considerable (albeit simple) arithmetic. With a large number of machines and orders this is such a tedious job that it is unlikely time will be available to do a thorough job. However, *nil desperandum*, help is at hand!

The information needed for each order is, firstly the floor-to-floor time (processing time plus set up and unloading times) on its preferred machine and, secondly, the ratio to this preferred time ("index") that represents the penalty of manufacturing the order on each non-preferred machine. Suppose, to take a simple example, that we have to schedule ten orders on five machines.

	A	B	C	D	E	F	G	H	I	J	K	L	M	N
1	ORD	M/C	〈----MACHINE INDEX-------〉					BEST LOAD		〈-----MACHINE LOAD--------〉				
2	NO.	TIME1	2	3	4	5		M/C	M/C	1	2	3	4	5
3														
4	1	10	1.00	1.20	1.80	2.50	〉〉〉〉〉	1	1	10.00	0.00	0.00	0.00	0.00
5	2	15	1.20	1.00	2.40	3.60	5.00	2	2	0.00	15.00	0.00	0.00	0.00
6	3	28	1.25	1.80	1.00	6.50	3.50	3	3	0.00	0.00	28.00	0.00	0.00
7	4	12	〉〉〉〉〉	1.15	1.25	1.00	2.80	4	4	0.00	0.00	0.00	12.00	0.00
8	5	20	3.25	4.75	〉〉〉〉〉	〉〉〉〉〉	1.00	5	5	0.00	0.00	0.00	0.00	20.00
9	6	15	1.10	1.20	1.70	1.00	1.45	4	4	0.00	0.00	0.00	15.00	0.00
10	7	14	1.40	1.05	1.00	1.10	1.35	3	3	0.00	0.00	14.00	0.00	0.00
11	8	17	1.27	1.00	1.44	〉〉〉〉〉	1.95	2	2	0.00	17.00	0.00	0.00	0.00
12	9	38	3.60	2.50	1.80	1.00	1.20	4	4	0.00	0.00	0.00	38.00	0.00
13	10	19	1.00	1.30	1.50	1.70	2.00	1	1	19.00	0.00	0.00	0.00	0.00
14														
15									NEEDED	29.00	32.00	42.00	65.00	20.00
16									AVAIL	40.00	40.00	40.00	40.00	40.00
17														
18									SPARE	11.00	8.00	0.00	0.00	20.00
19									O'LOAD	0.00	0.00	2.00	25.00	0.00
20														

The herring-bone patterns (〉〉〉〉〉) are generated by entering a very large index number (such as 99 999) to indicate that a particular order cannot be made on that machine and so there is no point in trying to schedule it on that machine. If you do then an enormous machine load is indicated, which is obviously incorrect.

Loading the orders onto the preferred machines results in a rather unbalanced machine load schedule. Rescheduling some of the work onto other machines, starting with the machine with the largest overload, could result in a much smoother loading schedule such as the following:

	A	B	C	D	E	F	G	H	I	J	K	L	M	N
1	ORD	M/C	〈----MACHINE INDEX-------〉					BEST LOAD		〈-----MACHINE LOAD--------〉				
2	NO.	TIME1	2	3	4	5		M/C	M/C	1	2	3	4	5
3														
4	1	10	1.00	1.20	1.80	2.50	〉〉〉〉〉	1	2	0.00	12.00	0.00	0.00	0.00
5	2	15	1.20	1.00	2.40	3.60	5.00	2	1	18.00	0.00	0.00	0.00	0.00
6	3	28	1.25	1.80	1.00	6.50	3.50	3	3	0.00	0.00	28.00	0.00	0.00
7	4	12	〉〉〉〉〉	1.15	1.25	1.00	2.80	4	2	0.00	0.00	0.00	12.00	0.00
8	5	20	3.25	4.75	〉〉〉〉〉	〉〉〉〉〉	1.00	5	5	0.00	0.00	0.00	0.00	20.00
9	6	15	1.10	1.20	1.70	1.00	1.45	4	5	0.00	0.00	0.00	0.00	21.75
10	7	14	1.40	1.05	1.00	1.10	1.35	3	3	0.00	0.00	14.00	0.00	0.00
11	8	17	1.27	1.00	1.44	〉〉〉〉〉	1.95	2	2	0.00	17.00	0.00	0.00	0.00
12	9	38	3.60	2.50	1.80	1.00	1.20	4	4	0.00	0.00	0.00	38.00	0.00
13	10	19	1.00	1.30	1.50	1.70	2.00	1	1	19.00	0.00	0.00	0.00	0.00
14														
15									NEEDED	37.00	42.80	42.00	38.00	41.75
16									AVAIL	40.00	40.00	40.00	40.00	40.00
17														
18									SPARE	3.00	0.00	0.00	2.00	0.00
19									O'LOAD	0.00	2.80	2.00	0.00	1.75
20														

The formula in J4 is @IF(J2=J4,B4*C4,O). All the formulae in the block J4 to N13 are similar. Juggling the schedule to iron out overloads on certain machines has resulted in a 7.2 % increase in total machine time but the result is a reasonably even machine load schedule. If cost is more important than actual time, then there is no reason why the schedule cannot be computed on the basis of machining cost instead of actual times, or even using both times and costs. It may be that you wish to keep a particularly expensive machine fully loaded and, if necessary, transfer work from cheaper but slower machines.... The scheduling criteria can be whatever you like and provided they are based on numerical logic VisiCalc can be of considerable assistance in deriving the best schedule without doing away with the knowledge and experience of the production planner.

Again, the formulae are so simple there's little point in including a detailed template listing. The above are just two examples of how VisiCalc can help in the field of production planning and scheduling – there are many more similar applications to be found in the average factory.

Forecasting

Manufacturing companies selling goods directly to the consumer market need to be able to balance sales demand against the economics of manufacturing. Ability to fill all orders from stock demands large stocks of goods on the shelf or small stocks and very quick response to a stock outage on the part of manufacturing. The former costs large sums of money in capital tied up in stocks. The latter costs a lot in setting up and tearing down machines to make small, urgent quantities. It would be much better to try to even out the fluctuations by anticipating sales demand and manufacturing to meet this anticipated demand. Not only does this help provide an even load on manufacturing, but it also helps keep stocks within reasonable limits and so keep the working capital to a minimum – assuming that the forecasts are acceptably accurate!

The easiest (and probably the least accurate) method of forecasting is to glance at past sales and to make a quick estimate of future sales – the "wet finger in the breeze" method. A slightly better way would be to look at the sales for the same period twelve months ago and use that figure to forecast this period's sales. Perhaps another method is to calculate the moving annual total for the current period, compare it with those for several immediately past periods to detect any trend and then to use the results to estimate next period's sales. A variation on the moving annual total method is that of a twelve month moving average which smooths out large fluctuations in sales but at the same time gives an indication of whether sales are increasing or decreasing and at what rate. A six month moving average is more responsive to changes in sales trend but is also more affected by large periodic variations in sales.

The problem with moving annual totals and moving averages is that generally they are not responsive to a rapidly rising or falling sales trend. All these methods give equal weight to each sales period which is taken into consideration. It would clearly be better to give decreasing weight to the older periods when forecasting the next period and this is what the method known as "exponential smoothing" sets out to do.

Exponential smoothing uses the formula

Forecast for period 2 = forecast for period 1
+ alpha × (actual for period 1 – forecast for period 1)

This could also be expressed as

New forecast = old forecast + alpha × old forecast error

Alpha is a measure of the sensitivity of the forecast – the higher the more sensitive to change – and lies in the range 0 to 1. Normally, a value of .5 is used. The various methods of forecasting are compared in the following table.

	A	B	C	D	E	F	G
1			MOVING	ANNUAL	6 MONTH	.5 EXP	.1 EXP
2		ACTUAL	ANNUAL	MOVING	MOVING	SMOOTH	SMOOTH
3	MONTH	SALES	TOTAL	AVERAGE	AVERAGE	F'CAST	F'CAST
4	==========	==========	==========	==========	==========	==========	==========
5	JAN	100				100	100
6	FEB	160				130	106
7	MAR	130				130	108
8	APR	90				110	107
9	MAY	180				145	114
10	JUN	170			138	158	120
11	JUL	130			143	144	121
12	AUG	140			140	142	123
13	SEP	100			135	121	120
14	OCT	130			142	125	121
15	NOV	110			130	118	120
16	DEC	170	1610	134	130	144	125
17	JAN	180	1690	141	138	162	131
18	FEB	190	1720	143	147	176	137
19	MAR	180	1770	148	160	178	141
20	APR	160	1840	153	165	169	143
21	MAY	200	1860	155	180	184	149
22	JUN	190	1880	157	183	187	153
23	JUL	210	1960	163	188	199	158
24	AUG		NA	NA	NA	NA	NA
25	SEP		NA	NA	NA	NA	NA
26	OCT		NA	NA	NA	NA	NA
27	NOV		NA	NA	NA	NA	NA
28	DEC		NA	NA	NA	NA	NA
29							

Taking row 16 as a representative row, the formulae involved are as follows:

```
Moving annual total :                       C16=@IF(B16<>0,@SUM(B5...B16),@NA
12 month moving average :                   D16=@IF(B16<>0,@SUM(B5...B16)/12,@NA
6 month moving average :                    E16=@IF(B16<>0,@SUM(B11...B16)/6,@NA
Exponential smoothing (alpha=.5) :          F16=@IF(B16<>0,.5*(B16-F15)+F15,@NA
                      (alpha=.1) :          G16=@IF(B16<>0,.1*(B16-G15)+G15,@NA
```

The graphs show that exponential smoothing with alpha = 0.5 does the best job of forecasting. None of the others produce acceptable results. Since only the formulae quoted above are of any significance, the worksheet template is not reproduced here.

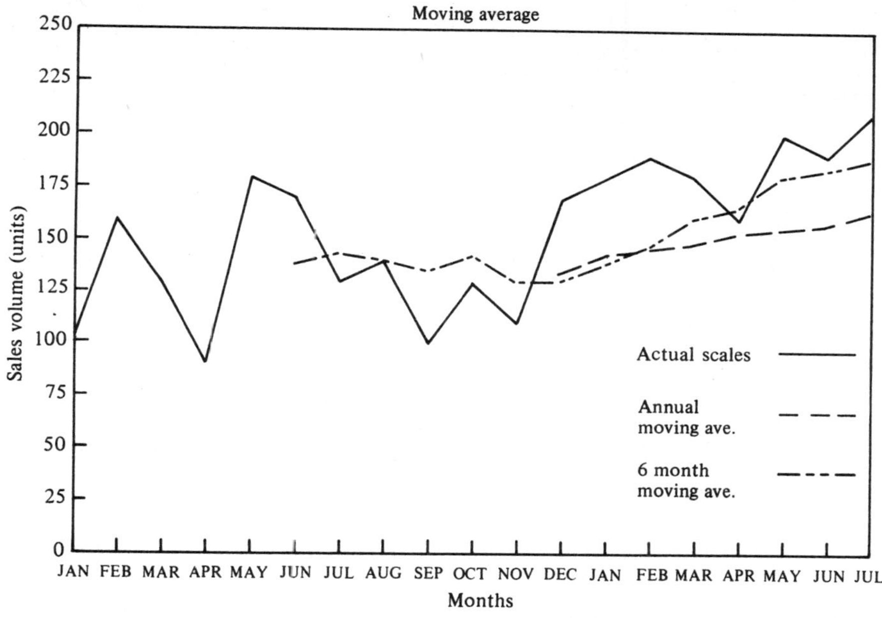

Moving average
250
225
200
175
150
125
100
75
50
25
0
Sales volume (units)
JAN FEB MAR APR MAY JUN JUL AUG SEP OCT NOV DEC JAN FEB MAR APR MAY JUN JUL
Months
Actual scales
Annual moving ave.
6 month moving ave.

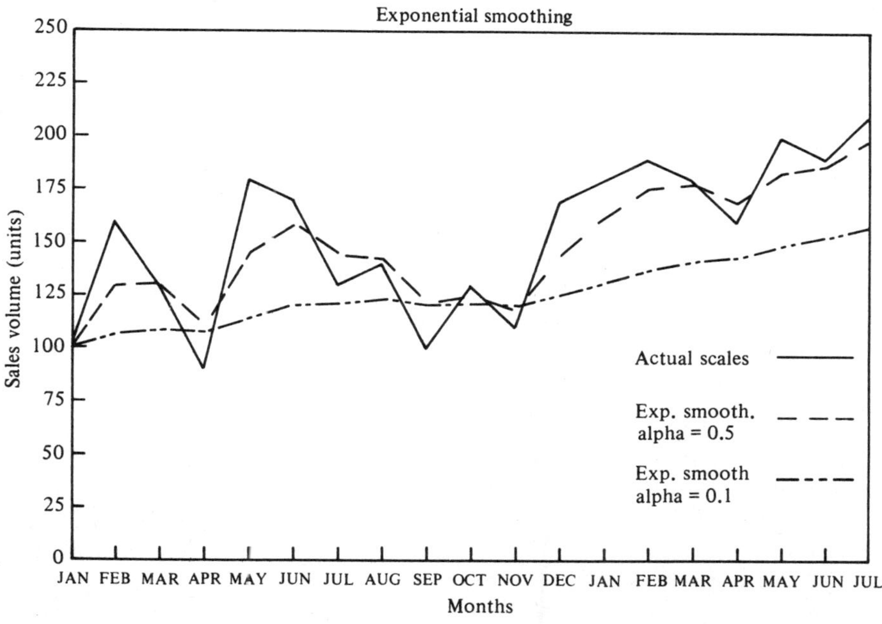

Exponential smoothing
250
225
200
175
150
125
100
75
50
25
0
Sales volume (units)
JAN FEB MAR APR MAY JUN JUL AUG SEP OCT NOV DEC JAN FEB MAR APR MAY JUN JUL
Months
Actual scales
Exp. smooth. alpha = 0.5
Exp. smooth alpha = 0.1

21

Technical templates

VisiCalc caters for technical calculations by providing transcendental functions such as sin, cos, tan, arcsin, arccos, arctan, log to base e, log to base 10 and natural exponent. The trigonometrical functions operate in radians, of course. Their accuracy can be tested by calculating the sine of an angle, then calculating the cosine of the result, then the tangent of this second result, then the arcsine, then the arccosine, then the arctangent. The answer should be the angle first thought of. Normally it isn't because of rounding errors in the algorithms which perform the calculations of the functions, but VisiCalc does rather better than even the best pocket calculator, as can be seen from the following test.

```
ANGLE(DEG)                                29

ANGLE(RAD)                     .50614548308
SIN                           .484809620268
COS                           .884763689753
TAN                            1.2214665579
ARCTAN                         .8847636898
ARCCOS                           .48480962
ARCSIN                        .506145482794

ANGLE(DEG                     28.9999999836
```

If the column width is reduced from 14 characters to 11 characters, the calculated results are displayed rounded to 9 significant figures, as follows:

```
ANGLE(DEG)                                29

ANGLE(RAD)                        .506145483
SIN                               .484809620
COS                               .884763690
TAN                               1.22146656
ARCTAN                            .884763690
ARCCOS                             .48480962
ARCSIN                            .506145483

ANGLE(DEG)                        29.0000000
```

This is a useful test of the capabilities of any trigonometrical calculator – not just of VisiCalc. The template for this test is as follows:

```
>B11:180*B9/@PI          >A6:''TAN               /W1
>A11:''ANGLE(DEG)        >B5:@COS(B4)            /GOC
>B9:@ASIN(B8)            >A5:''COS               /GRA
>A9:''ARCSIN             >B4:@SIN(B3)            /GC14
>B8:@ACOS(B7)            >A4:''SIN               /X!/X>A1:>A11:
>A8:''ARCCOS             >B3:@PI*B1/180
>B7:@ATAN(B6)            >A3:''ANGLE(RAD)
>A7:''ARCTAN             >B1:29
>B6:@TAN(B5)             >A1:''ANGLE(DEG)
```

A practical example of a trigonometrical calculation which is rather daunting when it has to be performed by hand, even with the assistance of a calculator, is that of resection. This is a method of finding out where you are by taking the bearings of three landmarks whose exact position is known. The three landmarks form a triangle with you somewhere inside that triangle.

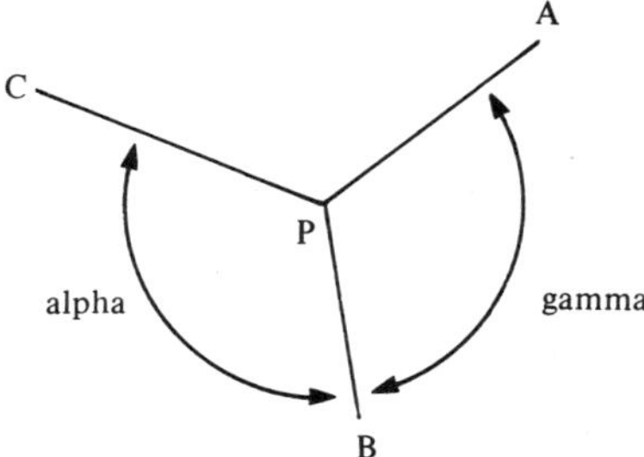

The positions of the three landmarks are known by their "eastings" and "northings" (i.e. the distances east and north of a fixed datum) and your position is calculated as eastings and northings from the same datum. The three landmarks are referred to as "A","B" and "C" and your unknown position as "P". The angle between PA and PB is called alpha and that between PB and PC is gamma. Ea and Na are the eastings and northings of point A, and similarly for points B and C.

The tangent of the bearing from P to B (formula 1) is

$$\frac{\text{Ea Cot(gamma)} - \text{Eb Cot(gamma)} - \text{Eb Cot(alpha)} - \text{Ec Cot(alpha)} - \text{Na} - \text{Nc}}{\text{Na Cot(gamma)} - \text{Nb Cot(gamma)} - \text{Nb Cot(alpha)} - \text{Nc Cot(alpha)} - \text{Ea} - \text{Ec}}$$

and similarly for the bearing from P to A.

The northing of P (Np) (formula 2) is

$$\frac{\text{Na Tan(PA)} - \text{Nb Tan(PB)} - \text{Ea} - \text{Eb}}{\text{Tan(PA)} - \text{Tan(PB)}}$$

The easting of P (Ep) (formula 3) is

$$\text{Eb} + (\text{Np} - \text{Nb})\ \text{Tan(PB)}$$

The VisiCalc worksheet looks something like this:

```
                  ENTRIES DECIMAL RADIAN  COT ANG1 COT ANG2 FORMULA1 FORMULA2 FORMULA3

        ANG1 DEG       221                                  276.7020 459.5274 170.6926
             MIN        30                                  216.7929 2551.102 217.8622
             SEC        10  221.5028 3.865953 1.130184
        ANG2 DEG        84                                           TAN PB   -2370.05
             MIN        45                                           1.276342 -1.09247
             SEC         6  84.75167 1.479196 .0918578

   EAST A          1500.61                    1695.965          .9062045 NORTH P EASTING P
   NORTH A         2499.12                    2824.465          -2.95975 2169.453 1439.992
   EAST B          1222.13                    1381.232 112.2621
   NORTH B         1998.76                    2258.967 183.6016TAN PA
   EAST C          1103.45                             101.3604.1838757
   NORTH C         2526.25  232.0557

   ----------------------------------
   ! EASTINGS OF POINT P        1439.992 !
   ! NORTHINGS OF POINT P       2169.453 !
   ----------------------------------
```

The template is as follows:

```
>E20:''-
>D20:/-
>C20:/-
>B20:/-
>A20:/-
>E19:'' !
>D19:+H11
>C19:''NT P
>B19:''GS OF POI
>A19:''! NORTHIN
>E18:'' !
>D18:+I11
>C18:''T P
>B18:''S OF POIN
>A18:''! EASTING
>E17:''-
>D17:/-
>C17:/-
>B17:/-
>A17:/-
>F15:+B15*E8
>B15:2526.25
>A15:''NORTH C
>G14:@TAN(G11)
>F14:+B14*E8
>B14:1103.45
>A14:''EAST C
>G13:'' TAN PA
>F13:+B13*E8
>E13:+B13*E5
>B13:1998.76
>A13:''NORTH B
>F12:+B12*E8
>E12:+B12*E5
>B12:1222.13
>A12:''EAST B
>I11:+B12+I4
>H11:+H6/H7
>G11:+G10-D5
>E11:+B11*E5
>B11:2499.12
>A11:''NORTH A
>I10:''EASTING P
>H10:'' NORTH P
>G10:@ATAN(G7)
>E10:+B10*E5
>B10:1500.61
>A10:''EAST A
>E8:1/@TAN(D8)
>D8:@PI*C8/180
>C8:(B8/60+B7)/60+B6
>B8:6
>A8:''    SEC
>H7:+G14-G7
>G7:+G3/G4
>B7:45
>A7:''    MIN
>H6:+H3-H4-B10+B12
>G6:'' TAN PB
>B6:84
>A6:''ANG2 DEG
>E5:1/@TAN(D5)
>D5:@PI*C5/180
>C5:(B5/60+B4)/60+B3
>B5:10
>A5:''    SEC
>I4:+I3*G7
>H4:+G7*B13
>G4:+E11-E13-F13+F15-B10+B14
>B4:30
>A4:''    MIN
>I3:+H11-B13
>H3:+G14*B11
>G3:+E10-E12-F12+F14+B11-B15
>B3:221
>A3:''ANG1 DEG
>I1:'' FORMULA3
>H1:'' FORMULA2
>G1:'' FORMULA1
>F1:'' COT ANG2
>E1:'' COT ANG1
>D1:'' RADIAN
>C1:'' DECIMAL
```

```
>B1:'' ENTRIES
/W1
/GOC
/GRM
/GC9
/X!/X>A1:>A1:
```

Linear Regression

	A	B	C	D	E
1	X	Y	XY	X*X	YCALC
2					
3	1	100	100	1	115.2
4	2	160	320	4	119.4
5	3	130	390	9	123.7
6	4	90	360	16	128.0
7	5	180	900	25	132.3
8	6	170	1020	36	136.6
9	7	130	910	49	140.8
10	8	140	1120	64	145.1
11	9	100	900	81	149.4
12	10	130	1300	100	153.7
13	11	110	1210	121	158.0
14	12	170	2040	144	162.2
15	13	180	2340	169	166.5
16	14	190	2660	196	170.8
17	15	180	2700	225	175.1
18	16	160	2560	256	179.4
19	17	200	3400	289	183.6
20	18	190	3420	324	187.9
21	19	210	3990	361	192.2
22		0	0	NA	
23		0	0	NA	
24		0	0	NA	
25					
26	190	2920	31640	2470	
27					
28					
29					
30	B=4.281				
31	A=110.9				
32					
33	Y=110.9+4.281 X				

The crucial formulae are:

```
A(in A31) = (B26-(B30*A26))/@COUNT(A2...A25)
B(in A32) = (C26*@COUNT(A2...A25)-(A26*B26)/
  (D26*@COUNT(A2...A25)-(A26*A26))
```

The complete template is as follows:

```
>E33:/FL"X
>D33:+B30
>C33:"+
>B33:+B31
>A33:"Y=
>B31:(B26-(B30*A26))/@COUNT(A2...A25)
>A31:"A=
>B30:(C26*@COUNT(A2...A25)-(A26*B26)/(D26*@COUNT(A2]b.127A25)-(A26*A26))
>A30:"B=
>E27:/-
>D27:/-
>C27:/-
>B27:/-
>A27:/-
>D26:@SUM(D2...D25
>C26:@SUM(C2...C25
>B26:@SUM(B2...B25
>A26:@SUM(A2...A25
>E25:/-
>D25:/-
>C25:/-
>B25:/-
>A25:/-
>E24:@IF(A24<>0,+B30*A24+B31,@NA)
>D24:+A24*A24
>C24:+A24*B24
>E23:@IF(A23<>0,+B30*A23+B31,@NA)
>D23:+A23*A23
>C23:+A23*B23
>E22:@IF(A22<>0,+B30*A22+B31,@NA)
>D22:+A22*A22
>C22:+A22*B22
>E21:@IF(A21<>0,+B30*A21+B31,@NA)
>D21:+A21*A21
>C21:+A21*B21
>E20:@IF(A20<>0,+B30*A20+B31,@NA)
>D20:+A20*A20
>C20:+A20*B20
>E19:@IF(A19<>0,+B30*A19+B31,@NA)
>D19:+A19*A19
>C19:+A19*B19
>E18:@IF(A18<>0,+B30*A18+B31,@NA)
>D18:+A18*A18
>C18:+A18*B18
>E17:@IF(A17<>0,+B30*A17+B31,@NA)
>D17:+A17*A17
>C17:+A17*B17
>E16:@IF(A16<>0,+B30*A16+B31,@NA)
>D16:+A16*A16
>C16:+A16*B16
>E15:@IF(A15<>0,+B30*A15+B31,@NA)
>D15:+A15*A15
>C15:+A15*B15
>E14:@IF(A14<>0,+B30*A14+B31,@NA)
>D14:+A14*A14
>C14:+A14*B14
>E13:@IF(A13<>0,+B30*A13+B31,@NA)
>D13:+A13*A13
>C13:+A13*B13
>E12:@IF(A12<>0,+B30*A12+B31,@NA)
>D12:+A12*A12
>C12:+A12*B12
>E11:@IF(A11<>0,+B30*A11+B31,@NA)
>D11:+A11*A11
>C11:+A11*B11
>E10:@IF(A10<>0,+B30*A10+B31,@NA)
```

```
)D10:+A10*A10
)C10:+A10*B10
)E9:@IF(A9<>0,+B30*A9+B31,@NA)
)D9:+A9*A9
)C9:+A9*B9
)E8:@IF(A8<>0,+B30*A8+B31,@NA)
)D8:+A8*A8
)C8:+A8*B8
)E7:@IF(A7<>0,+B30*A7+B31,@NA)
)D7:+A7*A7
)C7:+A7*B7
)E6:@IF(A6<>0,+B30*A6+B31,@NA)
)D6:+A6*A6
)C6:+A6*B6
)E5:@IF(A5<>0,+B30*A5+B31,@NA)
)D5:+A5*A5
)C5:+A5*B5
)E4:@IF(A4<>0,+B30*A4+B31,@NA)
)D4:+A4*A4
)C4:+A4*B4
)E3:@IF(A3<>0,+B30*A3+B31,@NA)
)D3:+A3*A3
)C3:+A3*B3
)E2:/-
)D2:/-
)C2:/-
)B2:/-
)A2:/-
)E1:''YCALC
)D1:''X*X
)C1:''XY
)B1:''Y
)A1:''X
/W1
/GOC
/GRA
/GFR
/GC6
/X!/X)A1:)A1:
```

Curvelinear regression

Curvelinear regression is performed in a similar way to linear regression, except that the raw data must be transformed in some way, such as by using their natural logarithms. For example:

X	Y	LN(X)	LN(Y)	LN(X)* LN(Y)	LN(X)↑2	LN(Y)↑2
333	150	5.808142	5.010635	29.10248	33.73452	25.10647
350	158	5.857933	5.062595	29.65634	34.31538	25.62987
366	165	5.902633	5.105945	30.13852	34.84108	26.07068
382	172	5.945421	5.147494	30.60402	35.34803	26.49670
397	178	5.983936	5.181784	31.00746	35.80749	26.85088
416	187	6.030685	5.231109	31.54717	36.36916	27.36450
437	196	6.079933	5.278115	32.09058	36.96559	27.85849
	AVERAGES	5.944098	5.145382			
	SUMS	41.60868	36.01768	214.1466	247.3813	185.3776

```
      E .0539937 G .0528621
      F .0551650 R .9997195
      M .9787673
  LN(B) -.672506
      B .5104277

  Y = .5104277 * X ↑    .9787673
```

The template is as follows:

```
)E22:/FL+C18
)D22:/FL'' * X ↑
)C22:+C20
)B22:''Y=
)C20:@EXP(C19)
)B20:''B
)G19:/FL
)F19:/FL
)C19:+D12-(C18*C12)
)B19:''LN(B)
)C18:+C16/C17
)B18:''M
)E17:+C16*C16/C17/E16
)D17:''R
)C17:+F13-(C13↑2/@COUNT(A3...A11)
)B17:''F
)E16:+G13-(D13↑2/@COUNT(A3...A11)
)D16:''G
)C16:+E13-(C13*D13/@COUNT(A3...A11))
)B16:''E
)G14:/-
)F14:/-
)E14:/-
)D14:/-
```

```
)C14:/-
)B14:/-
)A14:/-
)G13:@SUM(G3...G11
)F13:@SUM(F3...F11
)E13:@SUM(E3...E11
)D13:@SUM(D3...D11
)C13:@SUM(C3...C11
)B13:''SUMS
)D12:@AVERAGE(D3...D11
)C12:@AVERAGE(C3...C11
)B12:''AVERAGES
)G11:/-
)F11:/-
)E11:/-
)D11:/-
)C11:/-
)B11:/-
)A11:/-
)G10:+D10↑2
)F10:+C10↑2
)E10:+C10*D10
)D10:@LN(B10)
)C10:@LN(A10)
)G9:+D9↑2
)F9:+C9↑2
)E9:+C9*D9
)D9:@LN(B9)
)C9:@LN(A9)
)G8:+D8↑2
)F8:+C8↑2
)E8:+C8*D8
)D8:@LN(B8)
)C8:@LN(A8)
)G7:+D7↑2
)F7:+C7↑2
)E7:+C7*D7
)D7:@LN(B7)
)C7:@LN(A7)
)G6:+D6↑2
)F6:+C6↑2
)E6:+C6*D6
)D6:@LN(B6)
)C6:@LN(A6)
)G5:+D5↑2
)F5:+C5↑2
)E5:+C5*D5
)D5:@LN(B5)
)C5:@LN(A5)
)G4:+D4↑2
)F4:+C4↑2
)E4:+C4*D4
)D4:@LN(B4)
)C4:@LN(A4)
)G3:/-
)F3:/-
)E3:/-
)D3:/-
)C3:/-
)B3:/-
)A3:/-
)E2:''  LN(Y)
)G1:''LN(Y)↑2
)F1:''LN(X)↑2
)E1:''LN(X)*
)D1:''LN(Y)
)C1:''LN(X)
)B1:''Y
)A1:''X
/W1
/GOR
/GRM
/GFR
/GC9
/X-/X)A1:)A4:
```

Surveying

Land surveyors are frequently involved in the complex and tedious trigonometry of establishing the co-ordinates of a number of points on a traverse. This involves a series of measurements of distances and angles and the resolution of the inevitable small errors. The data required are the co-ordinates of the first and last stations of the traverse and of the reference objects at each end of the traverse, and the angles and distances to stations in between (see diagram.)

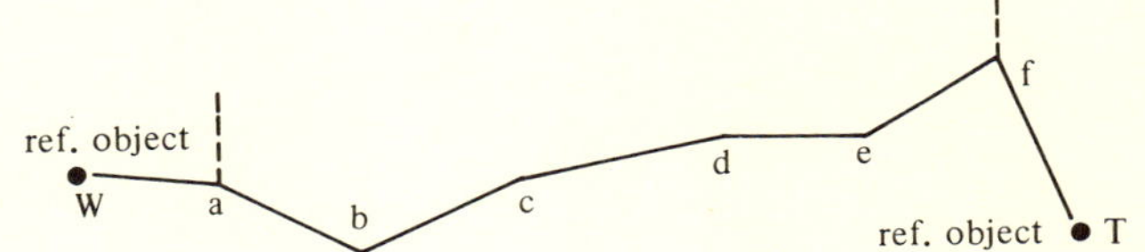

	ENTRIES	DIFF E	DIFF N	TAN BRG	BEARING	DEGREES
EAST A	41740.76					
NORTH A	11146.69	-100.98	101.03	-.999505	5.498035	315.0142
EAST W	41639.78					
NORTH W	11247.72					

		DECIMAL	DIF ANG	RADIANS		BEARINGS	BRG DEG	SINE	COSINE	DIFF E	DIFF N		EASTINGS	NORTHINGS
												STN A	41740.76	11146.69
STNA TO W	300	300												
A TO B	50.312	50.52222	110.5222	1.928977	BRG TO B	1.143826	65.53640	.9102246	.4141150	137.9536	62.76327			
DIST TO B	151.56											STN B	41878.71	11209.45
STNB TO A	50	50			REC BRG	4.285419								
B TO C	285.025	285.0472	235.0472	4.102348	BRG TO C	2.104581	120.5836	.8608875	-.508795	130.4331	-.770876			
DIST TO C	151.51											STN C	130.4331	-77.0876
STNC TO B	65.101	65.16944			REC BRG	5.246174								
C TO D	10.514	10.86111	305.6917	5.335326	BRG TO D	4.298315	246.2753	-.915489	-.402343	-138.733	-60.9710			
DIST TO D	151.54											STN D	-138.733	-60.9710
STND TO C	0	0			REC BRG	1.156722								
D TO A	233.523	233.875	233.875	4.081889	BRG TO A	5.238611	300.1503	-.864711	.5022699	-129.646	75.30533			
DIST TO A	149.93												-129.646	75.30533
NO OF STN	4										MISCLOSE		-41740.8	-11146.7
DISTANCE	604.54											RF 1:		0

The template is as follows:

```
>P44:/FI+B44/@SQRT((O42*O42)+(P42*P42))
>O44:/FR''RF  1:
>M44:/FR
>B44:+B20+B24+B28+B32+B36+B40
>A44:''DISTANCE
>H43:+H42/B42
>G43:+G42/B42
>F43:''BRG CORR
>P42:+P36-B10
>O42:+O36-B9
>N42:''MISCLOSE
>H42:+H39-G10
>G42:+G39-F10
>F42:''DIFF BRG
>B42:6
>A42:''NO OF STN
>I39:-G42/B42+G39
>H39:180*G39/@PI
>G39:@IF((G38+E39)>(2*@PI),(G38+E39)-(2*@PI),(G38+E39))
>F39:''BRG TO F
>E39:@PI*D39/180
>D39:@IF(C39<C38,360+C39-C38,C39-C38)
>C39:(B39*100-@INT(B39*100))*100/60+@INT(B39*100)-(@INT(B39)*100)/60+@INT(B39)
>B39:302.5906
>A39:''  F TO T
>G38:@IF(G35+@PI)(2*@PI),G35-@PI,G35+@PI)
>F38:''REC BRG
>C38:(B38*100-@INT(B38*100))*100/60+@INT(B38*100)-(@INT(B38)*100)/60+@INT(B38)
>B38:152.1806
>A38:''STNF TO E
>P36:(P32+M35)
>O36:(O32+L35)
>N36:''STN
>B36:86.732
>A36:''DIST TO F
>M35:(B36*K35)
>L35:(B36*J35)
>K35:@COS(I35)
>J35:@SIN(I35)
>I35:-G42/B42+G35
>H35:180*G35/@PI
>G35:@IF((G34+E35)>(2*@PI),(G34+E35)-(2*@PI),(G34+E35))
>F35:''BRG TO F
>E35:@PI*D35/180
>D35:@IF(C35<C34,360+C35-C34,C35-C34)
>C35:(B35*100-@INT(B35*100))*100/60+@INT(B35*100)-(@INT(B35)*100)/60+@INT(B35)
>B35:249.3758
>A35:''  E TO F
>G34:@IF(G31+@PI)(2*@PI),G31-@PI,G31+@PI)
>F34:''REC BRG
>C34:(B34*100-@INT(B34*100))*100/60+@INT(B34*100)-(@INT(B34)*100)/60+@INT(B34)
>B34:66.0401
>A34:''STNE TO D
>P32:(P28+M31)
>O32:(O28+L31)
>N32:''STN E
>B32:103.784
>A32:''DIST TO E
>M31:(B32*K31)
>L31:(B32*J31)
```

```
>K31:@COS(I31)
>J31:@SIN(I31)
>I31:-G42/B42+G31
>H31:180*G31/@PI
>G31:@IF((G30+E31)>(2*@PI),(G30+E31)-(2*@PI),(G30+E31))
>F31:'' BRG TO E
>E31:@PI*D31/180
>D31:@IF(C31<C30,360+C31-C30,C31-C30)
>C31:(B31*100-@INT(B31*100))*100/60+@INT(B31*100)-(@INT(B31)*100)/60+@INT(B31)
>B31:200.3336
>A31:''  D TO E
>G30:@IF(G27+@PI>(2*@PI),G27-@PI,G27+@PI)
>F30:'' REC BRG
>C30:(B30*100-@INT(B30*100))*100/60+@INT(B30*100)-(@INT(B30)*100)/60+@INT(B30)
>B30:6.0012
>A30:''STND TO C
>P28:(P24+M27)
>O28:(O24+L27)
>N28:''STN D
>B28:68.984
>A28:''DIST TO D
>M27:(B28*K27)
>L27:(B28*J27)
>K27:@COS(I27)
>J27:@SIN(I27)
>I27:-G42/B42+G27
>H27:180*G27/@PI
>G27:@IF((G26+E27)>(2*@PI),(G26+E27),(2*@PI),(G26+E27))
>F27:'' BRG TO D
>E27:@PI*D27/180
>D27:@IF(C27<C26,360+C27-C26,C27-C26)
>C27:(B27*100-@INT(B27*100))*100/60+@INT(B27*100)-(@INT(B27)*100)/60+@INT(B27)
>B27:348.3657
>A27:''  C TO D
>G26:@IF(G23+@PI>(2*@PI),G23-@PI,G23+@PI)
>F26:'' REC BRG
>C26:(B26*100-@INT(B26*100))*100/60+@INT(B26*100)-(@INT(B26)*100)/60+@INT(B26)
>B26:200.3012
>A26:''STNC TO B
>P24:(P20+M23)
>O24:(O20+L23)
>N24:''STN C
>B24:86.542
>A24:''DIST TO C
>M23:(B24*K23)
>L23:(B24*J23)
>K23:@COS(I23)
>J23:@SIN(I23)
>I23:-G42/B42+G23
>H23:180*G23/@PI
>G23:@IF((G22+E23)>(2*@PI),(G22+E23)-(2*@PI),(G22+E23))
>F23:'' BRG TO C
>E23:@PI*D23/180
>D23:@IF(C23<C22,360+C23-C22,C23-C22)
>C23:(B23*100-@INT(B23*100))*100/60+@INT(B23*100)-(@INT(B23)*100)/60+@INT(B23)
>B23:206.305
>A23:''  B TO C
>G22:@IF(G19+@PI>(2*@PI),G19-@PI,G19+@PI)
>F22:'' REC BRG
>C22:(B22*100-@INT(B22*100))*100/60+@INT(B22*100)-(@INT(B22)*100)/60+@INT(B22)
>B22:20.1005
>A22:''STNB TO A
```

```
>P20:(B4+M19)
>O20:(B3+L19)
>N20:''STN B
>B20:93.989
>A20:''DIST TO B
>M19:(B20*K19)
>L19:(B20*J19)
>K19:@COS(G19)
>J19:@SIN(G19)
>I19:+G42/B42+G19
>H19:180*G19/@PI
>G19:@IF((F4+E19)>(2*@PI),(F4+E19)-(2*@PI),(F4+E19))
>F19:'' BRG TO B
>E19:@PI*D19/180
>D19:@IF(C19<C18,360+C19-C18,C19-C18)
>C19:(B19*100-@INT(B19*100))*100/60+@INT(B19*100)-(@INT(B19)*100)/60+@INT(B19)
>B19:21.4056
>A19:''  A TO B
>C18:(B18*100-@INT(B18*100))*100/60+@INT(B18*100)-(@INT(B18)*100)/60+@INT(B18)
>B18:224.595
>A18:''STNA TO W
>P17:+B4
>O17:+B3
>N17:''STN A
>P16:''NORTHING
>O16:''EASTING
>M16:''DIFF N
>L16:''DIFF E
>K16:''COSINE
>J16:''SINE
>I16:''CORR BRG
>H16:''BRG DEG
>G16:''BEARINGS
>E16:''RADIANS
>D16:''DIF ANG
>A16:''DECIMAL
>B13:11662.92
>A13:''NORTH T
>B12:41826.36
>A12:''EAST T
>G10:180*F10/@PI
>F10:@IF(@ATAN(E10)<0,@IF(D10<0,@PI+@ATAN(E10),2*@PI+@ATAN(E10)),@IF(C10<0,@PI+@ATAN(E10),@ATAN(E10)
>E10:(B12-B9)/(B13-B10)
>D10:(B13-B10)
>C10:(B12-B9)
>B10:11565.35
>A10:''NORTH F
>B9:41852.31
>A9:''EAST  F
>B7:11045.77
>A7:''NORTH W
>B6:41639.78
>A6:''EAST  W
>G4:180*F4/@PI
>F4:@IF(@ATAN(E4)<0,@IF(D4<0,@PI+@ATAN(E4),2*@PI+@ATAN(E4)),@IF(C4<0,@PI+@ATAN(E4),@ATAN(E4))
>E4:(B6-B3)/(B7-B4)
>D4:(B7-B4)
>C4:(B6-B3)
>B4:11146.76
>A4:''NORTH A
>B3:41740.76
>A3:''EAST  A
>G1:''DEGREES
>F1:''BEARING
>E1:''TAN BRG
>D1:''DIFF N
>C1:''DIFF E
>B1:''ENTRIES
/W1
/GOC
/GRM
/GFR
/GC9
/X!/X>A1:>A1:
```

Closed traverses are catered for in a similar fashion.

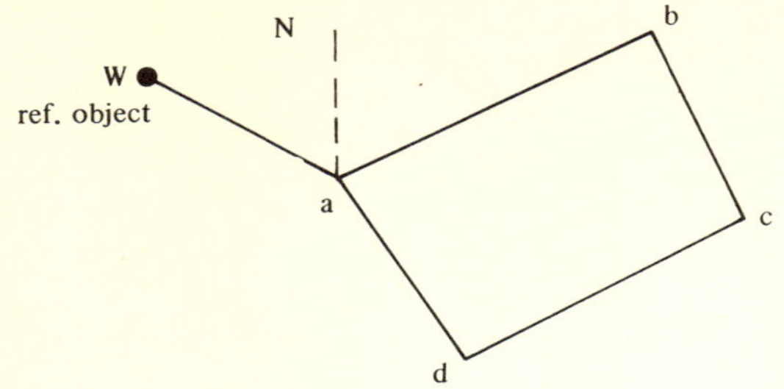

	ENTRIES	DIFF E	DIFF N	TAN BRG	BEARING	DEGREES
EAST	A41740.76					
NORTH	A11146.76	-100.98	-100.99	-.9999010	3.926941	224.9972
EAST	W41639.78					
NORTH	W11045.77					
EAST	F41852.31					
NORTH	F11565.35	-25.95	97.57	-.265963	6.023240	345.1062
EAST	T41826.36					
NORTH	T11662.92					

		DECIMAL	DIF ANG	RADIANS		BEARINGS	BRG DEG	CORR BRG	SINE	COSINE	DIFF E	DIFF N		EASTING	NORTHING
													STN A	41740.76	11146.76
STNA TO W	224.595	224.9972													
A TO B	21.4056	21.68222	156.6850	2.734669	BRG TO B	.3784251	21.68216	.3779600	.3694575	.9292476	34.72494	87.33906			
DIST TO B	93.989												STN B	41775.48	11234.10
STNB TO A	20.1005	20.16806			REC BRG	3.520018									
B TO C	206.305	206.5139	186.3458	3.252348	BRG TO C	.4891808	28.02800	.4896460	.4703135	.8824994	40.70187	76.37326			
DIST TO C	86.542												STN C	41816.19	11310.47
STNC TO B	200.3012	200.5033			REC BRG	3.630773									
C TO D	348.3657	348.6158	148.1125	2.585051	BRG TO D	6.215824	356.1405	6.216289	-.066846	.9977633	-4.61131	68.82970			
DIST TO D	68.984												STN D	41811.58	11379.30
STND TO C	6.0012	6.003333			REC BRG	3.074232									
D TO E	200.3336	200.56	194.5567	3.395654	BRG TO E	.1867007	10.69716	.1871659	.1860750	.9825355	19.31161	101.9715			
DIST TO E	103.784												STN E	41830.89	11481.27
STNE TO D	66.0401	66.06694			REC BRG	3.328293									
E TO F	249.3758	249.6328	183.5658	3.203828	BRG TO F	.2489362	14.26300	.2494014	.2468239	.9690603	21.40753	84.04854			
DIST TO F	86.732												STN F	41852.29	11565.32
STNF TO E	152.1806	152.3017			REC BRG	3.390529									
F TO T	302.5906	302.985	150.6833	2.629920	BRG TO F	6.020449	344.9463	6.020914							

NO OF STN 6

DIFF BRG -.002791 -.159906

BRG CORR -4.653-4 -.026651

MISCLOSE -.015357 -.027969

DISTANCE 440.031

RF 1: 13791

The template for this is as follows:

```
>030:/FI+B30/@SQRT((N28*N28)+(028*028))
>N30:/FR''RF  1:
>L30:/FR
>B30:+B14+B18+B22+B26
>A30:''DISTANCE
>028:+025-B4
>N28:+N25-B3
>L28:''MISCLOSE
>B28:4
>A28:''NO OF STN
>026:(021+L25)
>N26:(N21+K25)
>B26:149.93
>A26:''DIST TO A
>L25:(B26*J25)
>K25:(B26*I25)
>J25:@COS(G25)
>I25:@SIN(G25)
>H25:180*G25/@PI
>G25:@IF((G24+E25)>(2*@PI),(G24+E25)-(2*@PI),(G24+E25))
>F25:'' BRG TO A
>E25:@PI*D25/180
>D25:@IF(C25<C24,360+C25-C24,C25-C24)
>C25:(B25*100-@INT(B25*100))*100/60+@INT(B25*100)-(@INT(B25)*100)/60+@INT(B25)
>B25:233.523
>A25:''  D TO A
>G24:@IF(G21+@PI>(2*@PI),G21-@PI,G21+@PI)
>F24:'' REC BRG
>C24:(B24*100-@INT(B24*100))*100/60+@INT(B24*100)-(@INT(B24)*100)/60+@INT(B24)
>B24:0
>A24:''STND TO C
>022:(017+L21)
>N22:(N17+K21)
>M22:''STN D
>B22:151.54
>A22:''DIST TO D
>L21:(B22*J21)
>K21:(B22*I21)
>J21:@COS(G21)
>I21:@SIN(G21)
>H21:180*G21/@PI
>G21:@IF((G20+E21)>(2*@PI),(G20+E21)-(2*@PI),(G20+E21))
>F21:'' BRG TO D
>E21:@PI*D21/180
>D21:@IF(C21<C20,360+C21-C20,C21-C20)
>C21:(B21*100-@INT(B21*100))*100/60+@INT(B21*100)-(@INT(B21)*100)/60+@INT(B21)
>B21:10.514
>A21:''  C TO D
>G20:@IF(G17+@PI>(2*@PI),G17-@PI,G17+@PI)
>F20:'' REC BRG
>C20:(B20*100-@INT(B20*100))*100/60+@INT(B20*100)-(@INT(B20)*100)/60+@INT(B20)
>B20:65.101
>A20:''STNC TO B
>018:(013+L17)
>N18:(N13+K17)
>M18:''STN C
>B18:151.51
>A18:''DIST TO C
>L17:(B18*J17)
```

```
>K17:(B18*I17)
>J17:@COS(G17)
>I17:@SIN(G17)
>H17:180*G17/@PI
>G17:@IF((G16+E17)>(2*@PI),(G16+E17)-(2*@PI),(G16+E17))
>F17:'' BRG TO C
>E17:@PI*D17/180
>D17:@IF(C17<C16,360+C17-C16,C17-C16)
>C17:(B17*100-@INT(B17*100))*100/60+@INT(B17*100)-(@INT(B17)*100)/60+@INT(B17)
>B17:285.025
>A17:''  B TO C
>G16:@IF(G13+@PI>(2*@PI),G13-@PI,G13+@PI)
>F16:'' REC BRG
>C16:(B16*100-@INT(B16*100))*100/60+@INT(B16*100)-(@INT(B16)*100)/60+@INT(B16)
>B16:50
>A16:''STNB TO A
>O14:(B4+L13)
>N14:(B3+K13)>J13:@COS(G13)
>M14:''STN B>I13:@SIN(G13)
>B14:151.56>H13:180*G13/@PI
>A14:''DIST TO B
>L13:(B14*J13)
>K13:(B14*I13)
>G13:@IF((F4+E13)>(2*@PI),(F4+E13)-(2*@PI),(F4+E13))
>F13:'' BRG TO B
>E13:@PI*D13/180
>D13:@IF(C13<C12,360+C13-C12,C13-C12)
>C13:(B13*100-@INT(B13*100))*100/60+@INT(B13*100)-(@INT(B13)*100)/60+@INT(B13)
>B13:50.312
>A13:''  A TO B
>C12:(B12*100-@INT(B12*100))*100/60+@INT(B12*100)-(@INT(B12)*100)/60+@INT(B12)
>B12:300
>A12:"STNA TO W
>O10:+B4
>N10:+B3
>M10:''STN A
>O9:''NORTHINGS
>N9:''EASTINGS
>L9:''DIFF N
>K9:''DIFF E
>J9:''COSINE
>I9:''SINE  >H9:''BRG DEG
>G9:''BEARINGS
>E9:''RADIANS
>D9:''DIF ANG
>C9:''DECIMAL
>B7:11247.72
>A7:''NORTH W
>B6:41639.78
>A6:''EAST  W
>G4:180*F4/@PI
>F4:@IF(@ATAN(E4)<0,@IF(D4<0,@PI+@ATAN(E4),2*@PI+@ATAN(E4)),@IF(C4<0,@PI+@ATAN(E4),@ATAN(E4)))
>E4:(B6-B3)/(B7-B4)
>D4:(B7-B4)
>C4:(B6-B3)
>B4:11146.69
>A4:''NORTH A                >E1:''TAN BRG              /GOC
>B3:41740.76                 >D1:''DIFF N               /GRM
>A3:''EAST  A                >C1:''DIFF E               /GFR
>G1:''DEGREES                >B1:''ENTRIES              /GC9
>F1:''BEARING                /W1                        /X-/X>A1:>A1:
```

22

Fun With VisiCalc

For light relief, how about having fun with VisiCalc? After all, there's no reason why life should be too real and earnest! Try displaying your biorhythms, or playing noughts and crosses (otherwise known as tic tac toe).

Biorhythms

Page 1

		NO DAYS FROM BIODAY		WEEKDAY	DAY	MONTH	YEAR
BIRTHDAY							
DAY	23	0	13	4	19	12	1984
MONTH	8	1	13	5	20	12	1984
YEAR	1945	2	13	6	21	12	1984
		3	13	7	22	12	1984
BIODAY		4	13	1	23	12	1984
DAY	19	5	13	2	24	12	1984
MONTH	12	6	13	3	25	12	1984
YEAR	1984	7	13	4	26	12	1984
		8	13	5	27	12	1984
BIRTHYEAR	1945	9	13	6	28	12	1984
	9	10	13	7	29	12	1984
MOD JUL DAY	710709	11	13	1	30	12	1984
		12	13	2	31	12	1984
BIO YEAR	1984	13	14	3	1	1	1985
	13	14	14	4	2	1	1985
MOD JUL DAY	725072	15	14	5	3	1	1985
		16	14	6	4	1	1985
AGE IN DAYS	14363	17	14	7	5	1	1985

Page 2

```
MO.DA/WK        PHYSICAL                       SENSITIVITY                    INTELLECT
                       -+                                -+                           -+
12.1904********** *                 *******                       ********** *********
12.2005********                     **********                    ********** *********
12.2106******                       ********** **                 ********** *********
12.2207***                          ********** ****               ********** ********
12.2301*                            ********** ******             ********** *******
12.2402                             ********** *******            ********** ******
12.2503                             ********** *********          ********** ****
12.2604                             ********** *********          ********** **
12.2705*                            ********** **********         **********
12.2806**                           ********** *********          *********
12.2907****                         ********** *********          *******
12.3001*******                      ********** *******            *****
12.3102**********                   ********** ******             ***
 1.0103********** **                ********** ****               **
 1.0204********** *****             ********** **                 *
 1.0305********** *******           **********
 1.0406********** ********          *******
 1.0507********** *********         *****
```

The figure at the end of the date indicates the day of the week (Sunday = 1).

The template for biorhythms is as follows. It's a good example of the complicated arithmetic possible in VisiCalc, and of the use of trigonometrical functions.

```
>O20:/F*@SIN((((C20+B18-B14)/33)-@INT((C20+B18-B14)/33))*2*@PI)*10
>N20:/F*@SIN((((C20+B18-B14)/33)-@INT((C20+B18-B14)/33))*2*@PI)*10+10
>M20:/F*@SIN((((C20+B18-B14)/28)-@INT((C20+B18-B14)/28))*2*@PI)*10
>L20:/F*@SIN((((C20+B18-B14)/28)-@INT((C20+B18-B14)/28))*2*@PI)*10+10
>K20:/F*@SIN((((C20+B18-B14)/23)-@INT((C20+B18-B14)/23))*2*@PI)*10
>J20:/F*@SIN((((C20+B18-B14)/23)-@INT((C20+B18-B14)/23))*2*@PI)*10+10
>I20:+G20+(F20/100)+(E20/10000)
>H20:@IF(@OR(G20=1,G20=2),@INT((C20+B18-122.1)/365.25)+1,@INT((C20+B18-122.1)/35.25))
>G20:@IF(@OR(D20=14,D20=15),D20-13,D20-1)
>F20:+C20+B18-@INT(365.25*@INT((C20+B18-122.1)/365.25))-@INT(30.6001*D20)
>E20:@INT(7*(((C20+B18+5)/7)-@INT((C20+B18+5)/7))+.01+1
>D20:@INT(C20+B18-@INT(365.25*@INT(C20+B18-122.1/365.25))/30.6001)
>C20:1+C19
>B20:+B18-B14
>A20:''AGE IN DAYS
>O19:/F*@SIN((((C19+B18-B14)/33)-@INT((C19+B18-B14)/33))*2*@PI)*10
>N19:/F*@SIN((((C19+B18-B14)/33)-@INT((C19+B18-B14)/33))*2*@PI)*10+10
>M19:/F*@SIN((((C19+B18-B14)/28)-@INT((C19+B18-B14)/28))*2*@PI)*10
>L19:/F*@SIN((((C19+B18-B14)/28)-@INT((C19+B18-B14)/28))*2*@PI)*10+10
>K19:/F*@SIN((((C19+B18-B14)/23)-@INT((C19+B18-B14)/23))*2*@PI)*10
>J19:/F*@SIN((((C19+B18-B14)/23)-@INT((C19+B18-B14)/23))*2*@PI)*10+10
>I19:+G19+(F19/100)+(E19/10000)
>H19:@IF(@OR(G19=1,G19=2),@INT((C19+B18-122.1)/365.25)+1,@INT((C19+B18¬122.1)/35.25))
>G19:@IF(@OR(D19=14,D19=15),D19-13,D19-1)
>F19:+C19+B18-@INT(365.25*@INT((C19+B18-122.1)/365.25))-@INT(30.6001*D19)
>E19:@INT(7*(((C19+B18+5)/7)-@INT((C19+B18+5)/7))+.01+1
>D19:@INT(C19+B18-@INT(365.25*@INT(C19+B18-122.1/365.25))/30.6001)
>C19:1+C18
>O18:/F*@SIN((((C18+B18-B14)/33)-@INT((C18+B18-B14)/33))*2*@PI)*10
>N18:/F*@SIN((((C18+B18-B14)/33)-@INT((C18+B18-B14)/33))*2*@PI)*10+10
>M18:/F*@SIN((((C18+B18-B14)/28)-@INT((C18+B18-B14)/28))*2*@PI)*10
>L18:/F*@SIN((((C18+B18-B14)/28)-@INT((C18+B18-B14)/28))*2*@PI)*10+10
>K18:/F*@SIN((((C18+B18-B14)/23)-@INT((C18+B18-B14)/23))*2*@PI)*10
>J18:/F*@SIN((((C18+B18-B14)/23)-@INT((C18+B18-B14)/23))*2*@PI)*10+10
>I18:+G18+(F18/100)+(E18/10000)
>H18:@IF(@OR(G18=1,G18=2),@INT((C18+B18-122.1)/365.25)+1,@INT((C18+B18-122.1)/35.25))
>G18:@IF(@OR(D18=14,D18=15),D18-13,D18-1)
>F18:+C18+B18-@INT(365.25*@INT((C18+B18-122.1)/365.25))-@INT(30.6001*D18)
>E18:@INT(7*(((C18+B18+5)/7)-@INT((C18+B18+5)/7))+.01+1
>D18:@INT(C18+B18-@INT(365.25*@INT(C18+B18-122.1/365.25))/30.6001)
>C18:1+C17
>B18:@INT(365.25*B16)+@INT(30.6001*B17)+B8
>A18:''MOD JUL DAY
>O17:/F*@SIN((((C17+B18-B14)/33)-@INT((C17+B18-B14)/33))*2*@PI)*10
>N17:/F*@SIN((((C17+B18-B14)/33)-@INT((C17+B18-B14)/33))*2*@PI)*10+10
>M17:/F*@SIN((((C17+B18-B14)/28)-@INT((C17+B18-B14)/28))*2*@PI)*10
>L17:/F*@SIN((((C17+B18-B14)/28)-@INT((C17+B18-B14)/28))*2*@PI)*10+10
>K17:/F*@SIN((((C17+B18-B14)/23)-@INT((C17+B18-B14)/23))*2*@PI)*10
>J17:/F*@SIN((((C17+B18-B14)/23)-@INT((C17+B18-B14)/23))*2*@PI)*10+10
>I17:+G17+(F17/100)+(E17/10000)
>H17:@IF(@OR(G17=1,G17=2),@INT((C17+B18-122.1)/365.25)+1,@INT((C17+B18-122.1)/35.25))
>G17:@IF(@OR(D17=14,D17=15),D17-13,D17-1)
>F17:+C17+B18-@INT(365.25*@INT((C17+B18-122.1)/365.25))-@INT(30.6001*D17)
>E17:@INT(7*(((C17+B18+5)/7)-@INT((C17+B18+5)/7))+.01+1
>D17:@INT(C17+B18-@INT(365.25*@INT(C17+B18-122.1/365.25))/30.6001)
>C17:1+C16
```

```
>B17:@IF(@OR(B8=1,B8=2),B9+13,B9+1)
>O16:/F*@SIN((((C16+B18-B14)/33)-@INT((C16+B18-B14)/33))*2*@PI)*10
>N16:/F*@SIN((((C16+B18-B14)/33)-@INT((C16+B18-B14)/33))*2*@PI)*10+10
>M16:/F*@SIN((((C16+B18-B14)/28)-@INT((C16+B18-B14)/28))*2*@PI)*10
>L16:/F*@SIN((((C16+B18-B14)/28)-@INT((C16+B18-B14)/28))*2*@PI)*10+10
>K16:/F*@SIN((((C16+B18-B14)/23)-@INT((C16+B18-B14)/23))*2*@PI)*10
>J16:/F*@SIN((((C16+B18-B14)/23)-@INT((C16+B18-B14)/23))*2*@PI)*10+10
>I16:+G16+(F16/100)+(E16/10000)
>H16:@IF(@OR(G16=1,G16=2),@INT((C16+B18-122.1)/365.25)+1,@INT((C16+B18-122.1)/35.25))
>G16:@IF(@OR(D16=14,D16=15),D16-13,D16-1)
>F16:+C16+B18-@INT(365.25*@INT((C16+B18-122.1)/365.25))-@INT(30.6001*D16)
>E16:@INT(7*(((C16+B18+5)/7)-@INT((C16+B18+5)/7))+.01+1
>D16:@INT(C16+B18-@INT(365.25*@INT(C16+B18-122.1/365.25))/30.6001)
>C16:1+C15
>B16:@IF(@OR(B9=1,B9=2),B10-1,B10)
>A16:''BIO YEAR
>O15:/F*@SIN((((C15+B18-B14)/33)-@INT((C15+B18-B14)/33))*2*@PI)*10
>N15:/F*@SIN((((C15+B18-B14)/33)-@INT((C15+B18-B14)/33))*2*@PI)*10+10
>M15:/F*@SIN((((C15+B18-B14)/28)-@INT((C15+B18-B14)/28))*2*@PI)*10
>L15:/F*@SIN((((C15+B18-B14)/28)-@INT((C15+B18-B14)/28))*2*@PI)*10+10
>K15:/F*@SIN((((C15+B18-B14)/23)-@INT((C15+B18-B14)/23))*2*@PI)*10
>J15:/F*@SIN((((C15+B18-B14)/23)-@INT((C15+B18-B14)/23))*2*@PI)*10+10
>I15:+G15+(F15/100)+(E15/10000)
>H15:@IF(@OR(G15=1,G15=2),@INT((C15+B18-122.1)/365.25)+1,@INT((C15+B18-122.1)/35.25))
>G15:@IF(@OR(D15=14,D15=15),D15-13,D15-1)
>F15:+C15+B18-@INT(365.25*@INT((C15+B18-122.1)/365.25))-@INT(30.6001*D15)
>E15:@INT(7*(((C15+B18+5)/7)-@INT((C15+B18+5)/7))+.01+1
>D15:@INT(C15+B18-@INT(365.25*@INT(C15+B18-122.1/365.25))/30.6001)
>C15:1+C14
>O14:/F*@SIN((((C14+B18-B14)/33)-@INT((C14+B18-B14)/33))*2*@PI)*10
>N14:/F*@SIN((((C14+B18-B14)/33)-@INT((C14+B18-B14)/33))*2*@PI)*10+10
>M14:/F*@SIN((((C14+B18-B14)/28)-@INT((C14+B18-B14)/28))*2*@PI)*10
>L14:/F*@SIN((((C14+B18-B14)/28)-@INT((C14+B18-B14)/28))*2*@PI)*10+10
>K14:/F*@SIN((((C14+B18-B14)/23)-@INT((C14+B18-B14)/23))*2*@PI)*10
>J14:/F*@SIN((((C14+B18-B14)/23)-@INT((C14+B18-B14)/23))*2*@PI)*10+10
>I14:+G14+(F14/100)+(E14/10000)
>H14:@IF(@OR(G14=1,G14=2),@INT((C14+B18-122.1)/365.25)+1,@INT((C14+B18-122.1)/35.25))
>G14:@IF(@OR(D14=14,D14=15),D14-13,D14-1)
>F14:+C14+B18-@INT(365.25*@INT((C14+B18-122.1)/365.25))-@INT(30.6001*D14)
>E14:@INT(7*(((C14+B18+5)/7)-@INT((C14+B18+5)/7))+.01+1
>D14:@INT(C14+B18-@INT(365.25*@INT(C14+B18-122.1/365.25))/30.6001)
>C14:1+C13
>B14:@INT(365.25*B12)+@INT(30.6001*B13)+B3
>A14:''MOD JUL DAY
>O13:/F*@SIN((((C13+B18-B14)/33)-@INT((C13+B18-B14)/33))*2*@PI)*10
>N13:/F*@SIN((((C13+B18-B14)/33)-@INT((C13+B18-B14)/33))*2*@PI)*10+10
>M13:/F*@SIN((((C13+B18-B14)/28)-@INT((C13+B18-B14)/28))*2*@PI)*10
>L13:/F*@SIN((((C13+B18-B14)/28)-@INT((C13+B18-B14)/28))*2*@PI)*10+10
>K13:/F*@SIN((((C13+B18-B14)/23)-@INT((C13+B18-B14)/23))*2*@PI)*10
>J13:/F*@SIN((((C13+B18-B14)/23)-@INT((C13+B18-B14)/23))*2*@PI)*10+10
>I13:+G13+(F13/100)+(E13/10000)
>H13:@IF(@OR(G13=1,G13=2),@INT((C13+B18-122.1)/365.25)+1,@INT((C13+B18-122.1)/35.25))
>G13:@IF(@OR(D13=14,D13=15),D13-13,D13-1)
>F13:+C13+B18-@INT(365.25*@INT((C13+B18-122.1)/365.25))-@INT(30.6001*D13)
>E13:@INT(7*(((C13+B18+5)/7)-@INT((C13+B18+5)/7))+.01+1
>D13:@INT(C13+B18-@INT(365.25*@INT(C13+B18-122.1/365.25))/30.6001)
>C13:1+C12
>B13:@IF(@OR(B3=1,B3=2),B4+13,B4+1)
>O12:/F*@SIN((((C12+B18-B14)/33)-@INT((C12+B18-B14)/33))*2*@PI)*10
>N12:/F*@SIN((((C12+B18-B14)/33)-@INT((C12+B18-B14)/33))*2*@PI)*10+10
>M12:/F*@SIN((((C12+B18-B14)/28)-@INT((C12+B18-B14)/28))*2*@PI)*10
>L12:/F*@SIN((((C12+B18-B14)/28)-@INT((C12+B18-B14)/28))*2*@PI)*10+10
```

```
>K12:/F*@SIN((((C12+B18-B14)/23)-@INT((C12+B18-B14)/23))*2*@PI)*10
>J12:/F*@SIN((((C12+B18-B14)/23)-@INT((C12+B18-B14)/23))*2*@PI)*10+10
>I12:+G12+(F12/100)+(E12/10000)
>H12:@IF(@OR(G12=1,G12=2),@INT((C12+B18-122.1)/365.25)+1,@INT((C12+B18-122.1)/35.25))
>G12:@IF(@OR(D12=14,D12=15),D12-13,D12-1)
>F12:+C12+B18-@INT(365.25*@INT((C12+B18-122.1)/365.25))-@INT(30.6001*D12)
>E12:@INT(7*(((C12+B18+5)/7)-@INT((C12+B18+5)/7))+.01+1
>D12:@INT(C12+B18-@INT(365.25*@INT(C12+B18-122.1/365.25))/30.6001)
>C12:1+C11
>B12:@IF(@OR(B4=1,B4=2),B5-1,B5)
>A12:''BIRTHYEAR
>O11:/F*@SIN((((C11+B18-B14)/33)-@INT((C11+B18-B14)/33))*2*@PI)*10
>N11:/F*@SIN((((C11+B18-B14)/33)-@INT((C11+B18-B14)/33))*2*@PI)*10+10
>M11:/F*@SIN((((C11+B18-B14)/28)-@INT((C11+B18-B14)/28))*2*@PI)*10
>L11:/F*@SIN((((C11+B18-B14)/28)-@INT((C11+B18-B14)/28))*2*@PI)*10+10
>K11:/F*@SIN((((C11+B18-B14)/23)-@INT((C11+B18-B14)/23))*2*@PI)*10
>J11:/F*@SIN((((C11+B18-B14)/23)-@INT((C11+B18-B14)/23))*2*@PI)*10+10
>I11:+G11+(F11/100)+(E11/10000)
>H11:@IF(@OR(G11=1,G11=2),@INT((C11+B18-122.1)/365.25)+1,@INT((C11+B18-122.1)/35.25))
>G11:@IF(@OR(D11=14,D11=15),D11-13,D11-1)
>F11:+C11+B18-@INT(365.25*@INT((C11+B18-122.1)/365.25))-@INT(30.6001*D11)
>E11:@INT(7*(((C11+B18+5)/7)-@INT((C11+B18+5)/7))+.01+1
>D11:@INT(C11+B18-@INT(365.25*@INT(C11+B18-122.1/365.25))/30.6001)
>C11:1+C10
>O10:/F*@SIN((((C10+B18-B14)/33)-@INT((C10+B18-B14)/33))*2*@PI)*10
>N10:/F*@SIN((((C10+B18-B14)/33)-@INT((C10+B18-B14)/33))*2*@PI)*10+10
>M10:/F*@SIN((((C10+B18-B14)/28)-@INT((C10+B18-B14)/28))*2*@PI)*10
>L10:/F*@SIN((((C10+B18-B14)/28)-@INT((C10+B18-B14)/28))*2*@PI)*10+10
>K10:/F*@SIN((((C10+B18-B14)/23)-@INT((C10+B18-B14)/23))*2*@PI)*10
>J10:/F*@SIN((((C10+B18-B14)/23)-@INT((C10+B18-B14)/23))*2*@PI)*10+10
>I10:+G10+(F10/100)+(E10/10000)
>H10:@IF(@OR(G10=1,G10=2),@INT((C10+B18-122.1)/365.25)+1,@INT((C10+B18-122.1)/35.25))
>G10:@IF(@OR(D10=14,D10=15),D10-13,D10-1)
>F10:+C10+B18-@INT(365.25*@INT((C10+B18-122.1)/365.25))-@INT(30.6001*D10)
>E10:@INT(7*(((C10+B18+5)/7)-@INT((C10+B18+5)/7))+.01+1
>D10:@INT(C10+B18-@INT(365.25*@INT(C10+B18-122.1/365.25))/30.6001)
>C10:1+C9
>B10:1984
>A10:''YEAR
>O9:/F*@SIN((((C9+B18-B14)/33)-@INT((C9+B18-B14)/33))*2*@PI)*10
>N9:/F*@SIN((((C9+B18-B14)/33)-@INT((C9+B18-B14)/33))*2*@PI)*10+10
>M9:/F*@SIN((((C9+B18-B14)/28)-@INT((C9+B18-B14)/28))*2*@PI)*10
>L9:/F*@SIN((((C9+B18-B14)/28)-@INT((C9+B18-B14)/28))*2*@PI)*10+10
>K9:/F*@SIN((((C9+B18-B14)/23)-@INT((C9+B18-B14)/23))*2*@PI)*10
>J9:/F*@SIN((((C9+B18-B14)/23)-@INT((C9+B18-B14)/23))*2*@PI)*10+10
>I9:+G9+(F9/100)+(E9/10000)
>H9:@IF(@OR(G9=1,G9=2),@INT((C9+B18-122.1)/365.25)+1,@INT((C9+B18-122.1)/365.25))
>G9:@IF(@OR(D9=14,D9=15),D9-13,D9-1)
>F9:+C9+B18-@INT(365.25*@INT((C9+B18-122.1)/365.25))-@INT(30.6001*D9)
>E9:@INT(7*(((C9+B18+5)/7)-@INT((C9+B18+5)/7))+.01+1
>D9:@INT(C9+B18-@INT(365.25*@INT(C9+B18-122.1/365.25))/30.6001)
>C9:1+C8
>B9:12
>A9:''MONTH
>O8:/F*@SIN((((C8+B18-B14)/33)-@INT((C8+B18-B14)/33))*2*@PI)*10
>N8:/F*@SIN((((C8+B18-B14)/33)-@INT((C8+B18-B14)/33))*2*@PI)*10+10
>M8:/F*@SIN((((C8+B18-B14)/28)-@INT((C8+B18-B14)/28))*2*@PI)*10
>L8:/F*@SIN((((C8+B18-B14)/28)-@INT((C8+B18-B14)/28))*2*@PI)*10+10
>K8:/F*@SIN((((C8+B18-B14)/23)-@INT((C8+B18-B14)/23))*2*@PI)*10
>J8:/F*@SIN((((C8+B18-B14)/23)-@INT((C8+B18-B14)/23))*2*@PI)*10+10
>I8:+G8+(F8/100)+(E8/10000)
>H8:@IF(@OR(G8=1,G8=2),@INT((C8+B18-122.1)/365.25)+1,@INT((C8+B18-122.1)/365.25)
```

```
>G8:@IF(@OR(D8=14,D8=15),D8-13,D8-1)
>F8:+C8+B18-@INT(365.25*@INT((C8+B18-122.1)/365.25))-@INT(30.6001*D8)
>E8:@INT(7*(((C8+B18+5)/7)-@INT((C8+B18+5)/7))+.01+1
>D8:@INT(C8+B18-@INT(365.25*@INT(C8+B18-122.1/365.25))/30.6001)
>C8:1+C7
>B8:19
>A8:''DAY
>O7:/F*@SIN((((C7+B18-B14)/33)-@INT((C7+B18-B14)/33))*2*@PI)*10
>N7:/F*@SIN((((C7+B18-B14)/33)-@INT((C7+B18-B14)/33))*2*@PI)*10+10
>M7:/F*@SIN((((C7+B18-B14)/28)-@INT((C7+B18-B14)/28))*2*@PI)*10
>L7:/F*@SIN((((C7+B18-B14)/28)-@INT((C7+B18-B14)/28))*2*@PI)*10+10
>K7:/F*@SIN((((C7+B18-B14)/23)-@INT((C7+B18-B14)/23))*2*@PI)*10
>J7:/F*@SIN((((C7+B18-B14)/23)-@INT((C7+B18-B14)/23))*2*@PI)*10+10
>I7:+G7+(F7/100)+(E7/10000)
>H7:@IF(@OR(G7=1,G7=2),@INT((C7+B18-122.1)/365.25)+1,@INT((C7+B18-122.1)/365.25)
>G7:@IF(@OR(D7=14,D7=15),D7-13,D7-1)
>F7:+C7+B18-@INT(365.25*@INT((C7+B18-122.1)/365.25))-@INT(30.6001*D7)
>E7:@INT(7*(((C7+B18+5)/7)-@INT((C7+B18+5)/7))+.01+1
>D7:@INT(C7+B18-@INT(365.25*@INT(C7+B18-122.1/365.25))/30.6001)
>C7:1+C6
>A7:''BIODAY
>O6:/F*@SIN((((C6+B18-B14)/33)-@INT((C6+B18-B14)/33))*2*@PI)*10
>N6:/F*@SIN((((C6+B18-B14)/33)-@INT((C6+B18-B14)/33))*2*@PI)*10+10
>M6:/F*@SIN((((C6+B18-B14)/28)-@INT((C6+B18-B14)/28))*2*@PI)*10
>L6:/F*@SIN((((C6+B18-B14)/28)-@INT((C6+B18-B14)/28))*2*@PI)*10+10
>K6:/F*@SIN((((C6+B18-B14)/23)-@INT((C6+B18-B14)/23))*2*@PI)*10
>J6:/F*@SIN((((C6+B18-B14)/23)-@INT((C6+B18-B14)/23))*2*@PI)*10+10
>I6:+G6+(F6/100)+(E6/10000)
>H6:@IF(@OR(G6=1,G6=2),@INT((C6+B18-122.1)/365.25)+1,@INT((C6+B18-122.1)/365.25))
>G6:@IF(@OR(D6=14,D6=15),D6-13,D6-1)
>F6:+C6+B18-@INT(365.25*@INT((C6+B18-122.1)/365.25))-@INT(30.6001*D6)
>E6:@INT(7*(((C6+B18+5)/7)-@INT((C6+B18+5)/7))+.01+1
>D6:@INT(C6+B18-@INT(365.25*@INT(C6+B18-122.1/365.25))/30.6001)
>C6:1+C5
>O5:/F*@SIN((((C5+B18-B14)/33)-@INT((C5+B18-B14)/33))*2*@PI)*10
>N5:/F*@SIN((((C5+B18-B14)/33)-@INT((C5+B18-B14)/33))*2*@PI)*10+10
>M5:/F*@SIN((((C5+B18-B14)/28)-@INT((C5+B18-B14)/28))*2*@PI)*10
>L5:/F*@SIN((((C5+B18-B14)/28)-@INT((C5+B18-B14)/28))*2*@PI)*10+10
>K5:/F*@SIN((((C5+B18-B14)/23)-@INT((C5+B18-B14)/23))*2*@PI)*10
>J5:/F*@SIN((((C5+B18-B14)/23)-@INT((C5+B18-B14)/23))*2*@PI)*10+10
>I5:+G5+(F5/100)+(E5/10000)
>H5:@IF(@OR(G5=1,G5=2),@INT((C5+B18-122.1)/365.25)+1,@INT((C5+B18-122.1)/365.25)
>G5:@IF(@OR(D5=14,D5=15),D5-13,D5-1)
>F5:+C5+B18-@INT(365.25*@INT((C5+B18-122.1)/365.25))-@INT(30.6001*D5)
>E5:@INT(7*(((C5+B18+5)/7)-@INT((C5+B18+5)/7))+.01+1
>D5:@INT(C5+B18-@INT(365.25*@INT(C5+B18-122.1/365.25))/30.6001)
>C5:1+C4
>B5:1945
>A5:''YEAR
>O4:/F*@SIN((((C4+B18-B14)/33)-@INT((C4+B18-B14)/33))*2*@PI)*10
>N4:/F*@SIN((((C4+B18-B14)/33)-@INT((C4+B18-B14)/33))*2*@PI)*10+10
>M4:/F*@SIN((((C4+B18-B14)/28)-@INT((C4+B18-B14)/28))*2*@PI)*10
>L4:/F*@SIN((((C4+B18-B14)/28)-@INT((C4+B18-B14)/28))*2*@PI)*10+10
>K4:/F*@SIN((((C4+B18-B14)/23)-@INT((C4+B18-B14)/23))*2*@PI)*10
>J4:/F*@SIN((((C4+B18-B14)/23)-@INT((C4+B18-B14)/23))*2*@PI)*10+10
>I4:+G4+(F4/100)+(E4/10000)
>H4:@IF(@OR(G4=1,G4=2),@INT((C4+B18-122.1)/365.25)+1,@INT((C4+B18-122.1)/365.25))
>G4:@IF(@OR(D4=14,D4=15),D4-13,D4-1)
>F4:+C4+B18-@INT(365.25*@INT((C4+B18-122.1)/365.25))-@INT(30.6001*D4)
>E4:@INT(7*(((C4+B18+5)/7)-@INT((C4+B18+5)/7))+.01+1
>D4:@INT(C4+B18-@INT(365.25*@INT(C4+B18-122.1/365.25))/30.6001)
>C4:1+C3
```

```
>B4:8
>A4:''MONTH
>O3:/F*@SIN((((C3+B18-B14)/33)-@INT((C3+B18-B14)/33))*2*@PI)*10
>N3:/F*@SIN((((C3+B18-B14)/33)-@INT((C3+B18-B14)/33))*2*@PI)*10+10
>M3:/F*@SIN((((C3+B18-B14)/28)-@INT((C3+B18-B14)/28))*2*@PI)*10
>L3:/F*@SIN((((C3+B18-B14)/28)-@INT((C3+B18-B14)/28))*2*@PI)*10+10
>K3:/F*@SIN((((C3+B18-B14)/23)-@INT((C3+B18-B14)/23))*2*@PI)*10
>J3:/F*@SIN((((C3+B18-B14)/23)-@INT((C3+B18-B14)/23))*2*@PI)*10+10
>I3:+G3+(F3/100)+(E3/10000)
>H3:@IF(@OR(G3=1,G3=2),@INT((C3+B18-122.1)/365.25)+1,@INT((C3+B18-122.1)/365.25))
>G3:@IF(@OR(D3=14,D3=15),D3-13,D3-1)
>F3:+C3+B18-@INT(365.25*@INT((C3+B18-122.1)/365.25))-@INT(30.6001*D3)
>E3:@INT(7*(((C3+B18+5)/7)-@INT((C3+B18+5)/7))+.01+1
>D3:@INT(C3+B18-@INT(365.25*@INT(C3+B18-122.1/365.25))/30.6001)
>C3:0
>B3:23
>A3:''DAY
>O2:/FL''+
>N2:/FR''-
>M2:''+
>L2:/FR''-
>K2:''+
>J2:/FR''-
>C2:''FROM BIODAY
>A2:''BIRTHDAY
>O1:''LLECT
>N1:''     INTE
>M1:''TIVITY
>L1:''     SENSI
>K1:''ICAL
>J1:''     PHYS
>I1:/FR''MO.DA/WK
>H1:/FR''YEAR
>G1:/FR''MONTH
>F1:/FR''DAY
>E1:/FR''WEEKDAY
>C1:''NO DAYS
/W1
/GOC
/GRM
/GC11
/X!/X>A1:>A1:
```

Noughts and Crosses (Tic-tac-toe)

The empty frame before play commences. Player "1" plays player "9"

```
!=============================!
!      !!!!!!      !!!!!!     !
!-----------------------------!
!      !!!!!!      !!!!!!     !
!-----------------------------!
!      !!!!!!      !!!!!!     !
!=============================!

1 WINS      FALSE

9 WINS      FALSE

CHEAT?      FALSE
```

The game frame after a game...

```
!=============================!
! 1    !!!!!! 1    !!!!!! 1   !
!-----------------------------!
!      !!!!!! 9    !!!!!! 9   !
!-----------------------------!
! 9    !!!!!!      !!!!!! 1   !
!=============================!

1 WINS      TRUE

9 WINS      FALSE

CHEAT?      FALSE
```

...and after someone cheats!

```
!============================!
! 1     !!!!!! 1     !!!!!! 1     !
!----------------------------!
! 9     !!!!!! 9     !!!!!! 9     !
!----------------------------!
! 9     !!!!!!       !!!!!! 1     !
!============================!

1 WINS       TRUE

9 WINS       TRUE

CHEAT?       TRUE
```

The noughts and crosses template is as follows:

```
>C12:@IF(@AND(C8=@TRUE,C10=@TRUE),@TRUE,@FALSE
>A12:''CHEAT?
>C10:@IF(@OR(A1+C1+E1=27,A3+C3+E3=27,A5+C5+E5=27,A1+A3+A5=27,C1+C3+C5=27,
                         E1+E3+5=27,A1+C3+E5=27,A5+C3+E1=27),@TRUE,@FALSE
>A10:''9 WINS
>C8:@IF(@OR(A1+C1+E1=3,A3+C3+E3=3,A5+C5+E5=3,A1+A3+A5=3,C1+C3+C5=3,
                         E1+E3+E5=3,A1+C3+E5=3,A5+C3+E1=3),@TRUE,@FALSE
>A8:''1 WINS
>F6:''!
>E6:/-=
>D6:/-=
>C6:/-=
>B6:/-=
>A6:/-=
>F5:''!
>D5:''!!!!!!
>B5:''!!!!!!
>F4:''!
>E4:/-
>D4:/-
>C4:/-
>B4:/-
>A4:/-
>F3:''!
>D3:''!!!!!!
>B3:''!!!!!!
>F2:''!
>E2:/-
>D2:/-
>C2:/-
>B2:/-
>A2:/-
>F1:''!
>D1:''!!!!!!
>B1:''!!!!!!
/W1
/GOC
/GRA
/GFL
/GC6
/X-/X>A1:>A1:
```

A APPENDIX

Your computer

VisiCalc is available for a wide range of computers, not all of which have similar keyboard layouts. The Apple II, for instance, does not have four arrow keys for cursor movement, unlike the Apple IIe. Instead, the space bar is used to give dual functions to the two existing arrow keys. There may well be other differences as well between differing makes and models of computer. Some of these are described in the following paragraphs.

Apple II

To move the cursor to right or left, press the right or left arrow keys. To change to up or down, press the spacebar. The right and left keys now move the cursor down and up, respectively. The current direction of cursor motion is indicated in the top right hand corner of the screen by "!" for vertical and "-" for horizontal motion. To delete a character being typed into a cell, press the escape (marked "ESC"). To delete a character when editing, place the cursor just to the right of the character to be deleted and press ESC.

The Apple II keys do not repeat when held down. Either "woodpecker" the keys (i.e. tap them many times) or hold down the repeat key (marked "REPT") as well. The control key is marked "CTRL", but is needed only when editing the contents of a cell, and even then only rarely.

In the event of machine trouble, hitting "RESET" (or "CTRL-RESET") puts VisiCalc into storage mode (as if /S had been keyed) and so allows you to store the current file before quitting VisiCalc.

File names may be up to 30 characters long. All the letters and numbers are allowed in the file name, and most of the punctuation and other symbols are allowed except the comma. On a two disk drive machine, files are loaded from or saved onto the second drive by adding ",D2" to the file name. Drive 2 then becomes the current drive and all loads and saves from then on automatically are assumed to refer to that drive. To return to loading or saving to drive 1, append "D1" to the file name.

Apple IIe

The principal differences from the Apple II are that all keys repeat when held down and there are four arrow keys instead of only two.

Hewlett Packard 125

The HP 125 is a CP/M based computer. The keyboard is more complex than that of the Apples, but most of the extra keys do not function with VisiCalc. It has four arrow keys and one extra arrow key (marked with a diagonal arrow, pointing to the top left of the keytop) which sends the cursor to cell A1 (i.e. the "home" position or top left corner of the worksheet). All keys repeat when held down. The delete key is marked "DEL". The key marked "backspace" back spaces one character. The next character typed will overtype the previous character.

CP/M (Control Program / Microcomputers)

Most computers using the CP/M operating system have two disk drives as standard. The left-hand drive is usually referred to as the "A" drive and is the "master" drive from which the system is "booted" (i.e. started up). The right-hand drive (the "B" drive) normally contains the data disk. Sometimes the "A" and "B" drives are referred to as "0" and "1" instead.

File names are restricted to up to eight characters and, generally speaking, only letters and numbers are permitted, although this is not strictly true. Files to be saved on the disk in the "B" drive must have "B:" as the file name prefix. VisiCalc will add ".VC" as a suffix to ordinary VisiCalc files, ".PRN" to print files saved on disk, and ".DIF" to DIF (Data Interchange Format) files. Attempting to save data on a write protected disk (with a seal over the notch) will result in disaster in many cases since CP/M does not allow recovery from this situation. Opening the drive flap while VisiCalc is in use puts that drive into "read only" mode. This has the same effect as trying to save a file onto a disk write protected by a seal – disaster! There's no way of recovering data lost by such occurrences.

Floppy disks

Floppy disks (more correctly "diskettes") are flexible plastic disks coated with magnetic oxide which usually rotate at 300 rpm inside a tough plastic envelope. An oval cutout allows the recording head in the disk drive to touch the disk and record data or read it back. The disk is rotated by a cone and clamp arrangement which fits into the centre hole.

The disks can be damaged in several ways such as:

(i) being folded – they're flexible, but not that flexible!

(ii) being dented – don't write on the labels with anything sharp. Use a felt tip pen instead.

(iii) by dust – keep them in their envelopes when they're not in a drive.

(iv) by finger grease – don't touch the exposed oxide.

(v) by careless insertion in a drive – insert them gently and wait until the red "in use" light comes on before closing the drive door. This helps centre the disk on its drive cone. A chewed centre hole produces an unreadable disk.

(vi) by magnets – keep them off the top of the TV or monitor, and from under the phone!

Floppy disks come in a number of sizes and types. The 5.25 inch size is the most popular at present. It can be either single or double density and either single or double sided. Floppy drives can have either one or two recording heads. The Apple disks are single sided, single density (the cheapest!) and can hold around 128k (128,000) characters of data or programs. The HP disks are "single sided, double density" and cram twice as much onto one disk, thus needing a better quality disk. A double-sided disk has two usable surfaces. In a single-sided drive, this means that it can be used as if it were two separate single-sided disks by turning it over. The manufacturers did not make the disks with this in mind (and they probably wouldn't recommend such use) so they did not provide a matching "write enable" notch on the other edge. Careful use of a paper punch will cut a suitable notch. If money is tight, single-sided disks can be doctored in the same way and may well work satisfactorily, but the risk of failure is rather higher. Dual head drives have two read/write heads, one each side of the disk, and can read from or record onto both sides of the disk without the disk being turned over.

Printers

Printers come in many shapes and sizes. There are two principal types, dot matrix and fully formed character. Dot matrix printers create characters from a matrix of dots. Fully formed character printers operate more like a conventional typewriter by positioning the character to be printed at the correct print position and then hammering it onto the paper. There's a large difference in price and print quality. Most have at least two character sizes (10 chars./inch and 16.5 chars/inch) and two line spacings (6 or 8 to the inch). Unfortunately, the control codes which VisiCalc needs to send to the printer to invoke these character sizes, etc. vary from printer to printer so it's totally impracticable to attempt to give even a few of them here.

B APPENDIX

"Cribsheet" or ready reference guide

The "cribsheet" is divided into two sections – a summary of the commands, mostly beginning with a slash (/), and a list of VisiCalc's built in functions, all beginning with "@".

Command structure chart

/B Place cursor on cell to be BLANKed and type /B followed by pressing "return" or a cursor movement key. Pressing any other key cancels the command.

/C CLEARs the sheet (ready to start afresh) if Y is pressed. Any other key cancels the command.

/D DELETEs the row ("R") or column ("C") containing the cursor. The row or column is removed in its entirety and the rest of the sheet closed up. The rows or columns below or to the right of the row or column deleted are renumbered to preserve continuity of row and column identification and any formulae affected are adjusted completely automatically.

/E Allows the contents of the current cell to be EDITed. The arrow keys move the edit cursor along the edit line without changing anything. The character to the immediate left of the edit cursor can be erased by pressing "ESC" on the Apple ("Backspace" or "Delete" on some other computers). Insertions can be made at the cursor position merely by typing the character desired. Press "Return" to transfer the amended cell contents to the cell and exit from edit mode.

/F FORMATs a cell so that its contents will be displayed in a particular way. Any local format attributed to a cell using /F will take precedence over any global format attributed using /GF.

- D cancels the local format attributed to the cell. Any global format in force (the DEFAULT) will now take effect.
- G "GENERAL" – cancels all formatting (both local and global) attributed to the cell.
- I displays the cell contents as an INTEGER (i.e. without any decimal point or decimal places. Fractions are rounded to the nearest whole number only for display purposes. The complete number is used in any further calculations.
- L LEFT justifies text and numbers. Labels and numbers are displayed starting at the left boundary of the cell and any blanks needed to fill up the cell are placed to the right of them.
- R RIGHT justifies text and numbers. The extra blanks are placed to the left of the displayed characters.
- $ displays numbers rounded to two decimal places. ("Dollars & cents" or "pounds & pence" format).
- * rounds the number to the nearest integer and displays that many asterisks. Enables primitive bar-charts or histograms to be constructed.

/G acts "GLOBALly" – i.e. on the complete sheet.

- C changes the COLUMN widths. All columns have the same width which can be anything from 3 characters up to the full screen width of 40 or 80 characters.
- O sets the re-calculation ORDER to R ROW by row, or
  C COLUMN by column.
- R sets RE-CALCULATION either to
  A AUTOMATIC – i.e. the sheet is recalculated everytime a change is made, or
  M MANUAL – the sheet is recalculated only when ! is pressed. Useful when many changes have to be made to a large sheet.
- F FORMATs all cells not already formatted by /F. See /F for formats available.

/I INSERTs a row or column:

R INSERTs an unformatted ROW above the cursor position, and

C INSERTs an unformatted COLUMN to the left of the cursor position.

All the rows below and columns to the right of the inserted row or column are renumbered and all formulae affected are adjusted automatically.

/M MOVEs a row or column from the row or column comtaining the cursor to above a designated row or to the left of a designated column. When moving a row, both "from" and "to" cells must be in the same column but any column will do. Similarly, when moving a column, both cells must be in the same row, but it does not matter which row.

/P PRINTs the complete sheet or a specified part of it. The "printed" output can be sent to the actual printer, or it can be stored on disk for incorporation in a report prepared using a word processing package such as Applewriter II or Wordstar. The cursor is placed on the cell which will occupy the top left hand corner of the printout and /P is typed. The opportunity is then given to send a special stream of characters (starting with ") to the printer to "set it up" to print a specified number of characters per line, to tell it to expect a line feed at the end of each line (as well as the carriage return character) or to tell it no line feed character will be sent at the end of each line. If no special setup string is to be sent, merely press "return". The characters to be sent as a setup string vary from printer to printer, unfortunately. The bottom right hand corner of the printout is specified either by typing its co-ordinates or by placing the cursor on that cell and pressing "return". VisiCalc cannot work out whether the printout will fit into the width of the paper – that's your problem! You may have to split the printout into several strips, each of which fit onto the paper, which can then be taped side by side to form double width (or wider) printout.

/R REPLICATEs (reproduces) a cell or range of cells (all in one row or in one column) somewhere else on the sheet and adjusts any formulae involved as required. Replication can be one cell to one cell, one cell to part of a row or column, part of a row or column to part of another row or column, part of a row to part of a column or vice versa. The opportunity is given to specify individually whether each cell co-ordinate is to be adjusted to suit the destination row or column (R for "relative") or whether the cell co-ordinate should be used without adjustment (N for "no change"). Replication of a block (more than one row or column at a time) is not possible except when replicating one cell to many cells.
Place the cursor on the cell to be replicated (or the start of the range of cells) and type /R.
Now enter the cell co-ordinates of the end of the source range and type either a colon or press "return" (or just press return for a one-to-one or one-to-many cell replication).
Enter the cell co-ordinates of the start of the destination range followed by "return" for one-to-one or for one-to-many replication. For many-to-many replication, enter the cell co-ordinates of the start of the destination range and then press "return".

/S gives access to STORAGE of sheets on the disk drives.

S STOREs a sheet on disk under a user supplied name. This can be up to 30 characters long on the Apple, but CP/M based computers allow names of up to 8 characters only in length. If you are using two disk drives with VisiCalc in drive 1 (Apple) or in drive A (CP/M), then append ",D2" to the Apple file name, or precede the CP/M file name with "B:" to ensure the file is saved on the second drive.

L LOADs the sheet back into memory. It is usual to clear (/CY) the sheet before loading a fresh sheet from disk. If you've forgotten the file name, type /SL and then press the right arrow key to display the file names one by one. When the desired file name is diplayed, press "return" to load that file. If the file is on the second of two drives, type /SL,D2 (Apple) or /SLB: (CP/M) and then press "return".

D DELETEs the specified sheet from disk without loading it into memory first. The current sheet displayed on the screen is not affected even when the version on disk is deleted.

Q QUITs VisiCalc. Anything in memory is lost – so save it first! On the Apple, the VisiCalc disk can be removed and replaced by another disk. If the disk controller slot number is then typed, followed by "return", the system will be re-booted using the fresh disk.

I allows a brand new disk to be INITIALISEd or an old disk wiped clean ready for data to be saved to it. Not all versions of Viscalc have this facility.

#S specifies that the sheet (or part of the sheet) will be SAVEd as a DIF (Data Interface Format) file. Place the cursor on the top left hand cell of the range to be saved and type /S#S. Then specify the bottom right hand corner cell and press "return". The range of cells can be saved either row by row (R), or column by column (C). If it doesn't matter which way, just press "return".

#L re-LOADs a DIF file in a similar fashion. A file saved row-by-row can be re-loaded either row by row or column by column, and vice versa. Again, if it doesn't matter, just press "return". The names of the available DIF files can be displayed one by one in a similar fashion as when using /SL.

/T allows TITLEs such as column headings and/or row labels to be fixed so they do not scroll along with the rest of the screen.

H fixes all rows from the cursor up ("HORIZONTAL").

V fixes all columns from the cursor to the left ("VERTICAL").

B combines /TH and /TB ("BOTH").

N releases all title fixes ("NONE").

The cursor cannot be placed within the fixed title area except by jumping there by means of the goto (〉) function. /T can thus be used to protect cells against accidental alteration, but it is not a true cell protect facility.

/V displays the VisiCalc copyright notice and version number.

//W splits the screen at the cursor position, into two separate WINDOWs on the same sheet.

H splits the screen HORIZONTALly.

V splits it VERTICALly.

S ensures the two windows scroll in step (i.e. are SYNCHRONISED). If the screen is split vertically, then the two parts of the same row scroll together, and similarly for the columns when the split is horizontal.

U allows the two windows to be scrolled independently (i.e. UNSYNCHRONISED).

1 expands the ONE window containing the cursor to fill the screen.

; jumps the cursor between windows.

Separate global formatting may be applied to each window, so that each window may employ different column widths, for instance. However, the split window display cannot be printed as such.

/X is not an official VisiCalc command, but it can be used along with the goto (〉) command to place the cursor in a particular cell and the cell at the top lefthand corner of the worksheet. E.g. /X〉Z36 will place the cell Z36 and the cursor at the top left corner of the screen.

/- followed by a series of characters fills the current cell with that series of characters repeated as many times as is necessary to fill the cell. A good way to draw a horizontal line is to fill a cell with "-" or "=" and replicate the cell across the sheet.

〉 ("GOTO") followed by a cell co-ordinate jumps the cursor to that cell.

; JUMPs the cursor between windows when split sceen (/W) is in effect.

! FORCES RE-CALCULATION of the complete sheet. (See /GR for auto/manual recalculation option).

followed by "return" destroys the formula in a cell by replacing the formula with the value produced by the formula (i.e. it FIXes the value). It does this by placing the current displayed value on the edit line. The "return" then transfers this value into the cell and overwrites the formula, thus destroying it.

CTRL-E (control E) allows a formula or label currently being typed in to be edited, before being placed in its cell by pressing "return".

CTRL-C (control C) cancels editing invoked by CTRL-E.

VisiCalc functions

@SUM(list) totals the values specified in the list. The list may consist of individual cell co-ordinates, separated by commas, or may consist of a range indicated by a start cell, a dot (turned into an ellipsis (...) by VisiCalc) and an end cell. Labels (text) and blank cells, if included in the range, have numerical values of zero.

@COUNT(list) counts the number of values in the list. Labels and blank cells are ignored.

@MAX(list) returns the highest value in the list of cell co-ordinates. Labels and blanks count as zeroes.

@MIN(list) returns the lowest value in the list. Labels and blanks count as zeroes.

@AVERAGE(list) calculates the average of the values in the list. Labels and blanks are ignored.

@NPV(rate,range) calculates the net present value of a series of periodic cash flows, using the specified discount rate. The range consists of the first and last cell co-ordinates of the range of cells containing the cash flows.

@CHOOSE(N,range) chooses the Nth entry from the indicated range. The range may be a series of discrete cells, or may be a range indicated by start and end cells.

@LOOKUP(N,range) examines the range until a number larger than N is found. VisiCalc then steps back one cell and picks up the value in the cell in the immediately adjacent column (or row).

@NA produces a "not available" value which in turn produces the same value when used in subsequent expressions.

@ERROR produces "error" in a similar fashion to @NA.

@PI gives the value of π to 10 decimal places.

@ABS(N) results in the absolute value of N, i.e. any negative sign is converted to positive.

@INT(N) removes all decimal places to give a whole number, i.e. an integer.

@SQRT(N) gives the square root of N.

@IF(test,action 1,action 2) allows alternative courses of action to be taken. If the result of the test is true, then action 1 is taken. If false, then action 2 is taken.

@AND(test 1, test 2, etc.) can be used to combine tests within the @IF function. Only if all the tests are true will action 1 be taken.

@OR(test 1, test 2, etc.) can also be used to combine tests. If any one of them is true then action 1 is taken.

@NOT(expression) reverses the truth or falsity of the expression in parentheses. Unless you are skilled in Boolean logic then it's probably a good idea to leave this function alone!

@TRUE results in the Boolean value 'true'.

@FALSE results in the Boolean value 'false'.

@ISNA(N) results in 'true' if N has the value 'NA'.

@ISERROR(N) results in 'true' if N has the value 'ERROR'.

@EXP(N) gives the natural exponential of N.

@LN(N) gives the natural logarithm of N.

@LOG10(N) gives the log to base 10 of N.

@SIN(angle) gives the sine of the angle. The angle must be expressed in radians.

@COS(angle) gives the cosine of the angle.

@TAN(angle) gives the tangent of the angle.

@ASIN(N) gives the arcsine of N.

@ACOS(N) gives the arcosine of N.

@ATAN(N) gives the arctangent of N.

Comparison Operators

> greater than.
< less than.
>= greater than or equal to. i.e. not less than.
<= less than or equal to, i.e. not greater than.
= equal to.
<> not equal to, i.e. less than or greater than.

Calculation Hierarchy

VisiCalc evaluates arithmetic expressions strictly from left to right. If this sequence must be altered then portions of the expression must be enclosed within parentheses. VisiCalc then examines the expression for the innermost set of parentheses, evaluates the expression within them strictly from left to right, then looks for the next innermost set of parentheses and so on. This means that the expression 9 + 6 / 3 evaluates to 5, but 9 + (6 / 3) evaluates to 11.

C APPENDIX

VisiCalc has no provision for printing out the formulae used, nor does it allow for columns of varying widths. Fortunately, VisiCalc files can be processed by programs written in either Applesoft or other BASICs.

VisiCalc formulae printer

Save the VisiCalc file using /SS and then run this BASIC program.

```
 10 REM *******************************
 20 REM *  VISICALC FORMULA PRINTER    *
 30 REM *                              *
 40 REM *     VERSION OF MAY 1983      *
 50 REM *         BOB MOULD            *
 60 REM *        (APPLESOFT)           *
 70 REM *******************************
 80 HOME :D$ = CHR$ (4)
 90 INPUT ''WHICH FILE ? '';FILE$
100 PRINT
110 PRINT D$''OPEN''FILE$
120 PRINT D$''READ''FILE$
130 GOSUB 460: REM  SET PRINT PARAMETERS
140 GOSUB 540: REM  INITIALISE PRINTOUT
150 REM  READ FILE ********************
160 GET ST$
170 ONERR  GOTO 210
180 IF ST$ = CHR$ (13) THEN 230
190 F$ = F$ + ST$
200 GOTO 160
210 IF  PEEK (222) = 5 THEN 410
220 PRINT ''ERROR CODE ''; PEEK (222);
    '' IN LINE ''; PEEK (218) +
    PEEK (219) * 256: END
230 REM  PRINTOUT *********************
240 X = INT (( LEN (F$) + 10) / 10) * 10
250 F$ = F$ + ''            ''
260 F$ = LEFT$ (F$,X)
270 IF LEN (L$) + LEN (F$) > = CHARS
    THEN 320
280 L$ = L$ + F$
290 F$ = '' ''
300 GOTO 160
310 GOSUB 580
320 IF LEN (L$) < = CHARS THEN 360
330 GOSUB 580
340 PRINT  LEFT$ (L$,CHARS)
350 L$ = MARGIN$ + RIGHT$ (L$, LEN (L$)
    - CHARS)
360 GOSUB 580
370 PRINT L$
380 L$ = MARGIN$ + F$
390 F$ = '' ''
400 GOTO 160
410 GOSUB 770
420 END
450 REM  SUB-ROUTINES FOLLOW ++++++++++++
460 REM  PRINT PARAMETERS *************
470 PAGE = 55: REM  LINES / PAGE
480 LPAG = 66: REM  PAPER LENGTH
490 CHARS = 80: REM  CHARS / LINE
500 MARGIN$ = "    "
510 L$ = MARGIN$
520 LINCOUNT = 99
530 RETURN
540 REM  INITIALISE PRINTER *************
550 PR#1
560 PRINT  CHR$ (9)''80N'' CHR$ (29)
570 RETURN
580 REM   TEST FOR END OF PAGE **********
590 GOSUB 540
600 IF PAGE > = LINCOUNT THEN LINCOUNT
    = LINCOUNT + 1: RETURN
610 FOR K = LINCOUNT + 1 TO LPAG
620 PRINT CHR$ (10)
630 NEXT K
640 REM   HEAD UP NEW PAGE **************
650 IF PGNO = 0 THEN 670
660 GET CHAR$
670 PGNO = PGNO + 1
680 GOSUB 540
690 PRINT MARGIN$;
700 PRINT ''VISICALC FORMULAE FOR ''';FILE$;
    ''' - PAGE '' ;PGNO
710 PRINT MARGIN$;
720 PRINT ''======================'';
730 FOR J = 1 TO LEN (FILE$):PRINT ''='';:
    NEXT J: PRINT '' ''
740 PRINT '' ''
750 LINCOUNT = 4
760 RETURN
770 REM   RUN OUT TO END OF LAST PAGE ***
780 GOSUB 540
790 IF LEN (F$) = 0 THEN 810
800 PRINT L$ + F$
810 FOR J = LINCOUNT + 1 TO LPAG - 1
    : PRINT '' '': NEXT J
820 PRINT '' ''
830 PR# 0
840 RETURN
```

```
10  REM * ****************************
20  REM *  VISICALC FORMULA PRINTER   *
30  REM *                             *
40  REM *        OCTOBER 1983         *
50  REM *         BOB MOULD           *
60  REM *     (MICROSOFT BASIC)       *
70  REM * ****************************
80  HOME
90  INPUT ''WHICH FILE ''; FILE$
100 PRINT
110 OPEN ''IN'',#1,FILE$
120 GOSUB 380: REM  SET PRINT PARAMETERS
130 GOSUB 460: REM  INITIALISE PRINTOUT
140 REM  READ FILE
150 IF EOF(1) THEN 350
160 LINE INPUT#1,F$
170 REM  PRINTOUT
180 X = INT (( LEN (F$) + 10) / 10) * 10
190 F$ = F$ + ''          ''
200 F$ = LEFT$ (F$,X)
210 IF LEN (L$) + LEN (F$) 〉= CHARS
    THEN 250
220 L$ = L$ + F$
230 F$ = '' ''
240 GOTO 150
250 IF LEN (L$) 〈 = CHARS THEN 300
260 GOSUB 480
270 LPRINT LEFT$(L$,CHARS)
290 L$ = MARGIN$ + RIGHT$ (L$, LEN (L$)
    - CHARS)
300 GOSUB 480
310 LPRINT L$
320 L$ = MARGIN$ + F$
330 F$='' ''
340 GOTO 150
350 GOSUB 660
360 CLOSE#1: END
370 REM  SUB-ROUTINES FOLLOW...
380 REM  PRINT PARAMETERS
390 PAGE = 55: REM  LINES / PAGE
400 LPAG = 66: REM  PAPER LENGTH
410 CHARS = 80: REM  CHARS / LINE
420 MARGIN$ = ''          ''
430 L$ = MARGIN$
440 LINCOUNT = 99
450 RETURN
460 REM  INITIALISE PRINTER
465 REM  PRINTER INITIALISATION STRING
470 RETURN
480 REM  TEST FOR END OF PAGE
490 GOSUB 460
500 IF PAGE 〉= LINCOUNT THEN LINCOUNT
    = LINCOUNT + 1: RETURN
510 FOR K = LINCOUNT + 1 TO LPAG
520 LPRINT CHR$(10)
530 NEXT K
540 REM  HEAD UP NEW PAGE
550 IF PGNO = 0 THEN 560
560 PGNO = PGNO + 1
570 GOSUB 460
580 LPRINT MARGIN$;
590 LPRINT ''VISICALC FORMULAE FOR '''; FILE$ ;
    ''' - PAGE '' ; PGNO
600 LPRINT MARGIN$;
610 LPRINT ''========================'';
620 FOR J = 1 TO LEN (FILE$): LPRINT ''='';
    : NEXT J: LPRINT '' ''
630 LPRINT '' ''
640 LINCOUNT = 4
650 RETURN
660 REM  RUN OUT TO END OF LAST PAGE
670 GOSUB 460
680 IF LEN (F$) = 0 THEN 700
690 LPRINT L$ + F$
700 FOR J = LINCOUNT + 1 TO LPAG - 1:
    LPRINT '' '': NEXT J
710 LPRINT  ''  ''  : RETURN
```

Variable width columns

Variable width columns can be achieved by setting the VisiCalc column width to the widest required by the worksheet, saving the displayed results using /PF and then processing the results using the BASIC program VISIPRNT. The program will ask for:

(i)	VisiCalc printout file name	
(ii)	Number of VisiCalc columns	
(iii)	Current VisiCalc column width	
(iv)	Letter(s) of column(s) to be narrowed	) repeat
(v)	New width(s)	) as
(vi)	Left or right truncation	) needed

```
10  REM *********************
20  REM *                   *
30  REM *     VISIPRINT     *
40  REM *     BOB MOULD     *
50  REM *    OCTOBER 1983   *
60  REM *    (APPLESOFT)    *
70  REM *********************
80  REM
90  REM PROVIDES VARIABLE
100 REM  COLUMN WIDTHS FOR
110 REM  VISICALC PRINTOUTS BY
120 REM  TRUNCATING CELL CONTENTS
130 REM
140 REM  .......................
150 DIM  CD$(63),CW(63),TR$(63)
160 REM  READ VALID COLUMN DESIGNATORS
170 FOR J = 1 TO 26
180 READ CD$(J)
190 NEXT J
200 DATA  A,B,C,D,E,F,G,H,I,J,K,L,M,
          N,O,P,Q,R,S,T,U,V,W,X,Y,Z
210 FOR J = 27 TO 52
220 CD$(J) = ''A'' + CD$(J - 26)
230 NEXT J
```

```
240  FOR J = 53 TO 63
250  CD$(J) = ''B'' + CD$(J - 52)
260  NEXT J
270  REM
280  REM .......................
290  HOME
300  PRINT ''WHAT'S VISICALC PRINTOUT
                  FILE NAME ''
310  INPUT F$
320  REM
330  REM  ASK FOR CURRENT NO.OF
340  REM  COLUMNS AND COLUMN
350  REM  WIDTH.
360  REM
370  PRINT ''HOW MANY COLUMNS '';
380  INPUT LL
390  IF LL > 0 THEN 430
400  PRINT : PRINT ''STOP MUCKING ABOUT!''
410  PRINT
420  GOTO 370
430  REM  GET CURRENT COLUMN WIDTH
440  PRINT
450  PRINT ''WHAT'S CURRENT COLUMN WIDTH ''
460  INPUT CW
470  REM  CALC CHARS IN LINE
480  CL = LL * CW
490  REM  SETUP ARRAY OF COLS AND WIDTHS
500  FOR J = 1 TO LL
510  CW(J) = CW
520  NEXT J
530  REM  GET NEW COLUMN WIDTHS
540  REM  ASSUME WIDTH=CURRENT WIDTH
550  REM  UNLESS OTHERWISE INPUT.
560  PRINT
570  PRINT ''GIVE THE FOLLOWING ONLY FOR THOSE''
580  PRINT ''COLUMNS TO BE CHANGED :''
590  PRINT
600  PRINT ''COLUMN LETTER(S)''
610  PRINT ''NEW COLUMN WIDTH''
620  PRINT ''TRUNCATE ON LEFT OR RIGHT.''
630  PRINT
640  PRINT ''COLUMN (A TO BK)     :''
650  PRINT ''('END' TO EXIT)      :'';
660  INPUT NC$
670  IF NC$ = ''END'' THEN 900
680  PRINT ''NEW WIDTH          :'';
690  INPUT NW
700  PRINT ''TRUNCATE (L) OR (R) :'';
710  INPUT TR$
720  FOR J = 1 TO 63
730  IF NC$ = CD$(J) THEN 790
740  NEXT J
750  PRINT
760  PRINT  CHR$ (7)
770  PRINT ''INVALID COLUMN LETTER(S)''
780  GOTO 640
790  TR$(J) = TR$
800  FOR J = 1 TO LEN (NC$)
810  CN = 0
820  CN$ = MID$ (NC$,J,1)
830  IF CN$ = '' '' THEN 870
840  CN = CN + ASC (CN$) - 64
850  CN$ = '' ''
860  NEXT J
870  CW(CN) = NW
880  GOTO 630
890  REM  OPEN VISICALC PRINTOUT FILE
900  PRINT  CHR$ (4);''OPEN'';F$
910  PRINT CHR$ (4);''READ'';F$
920  ONERR  GOTO 1140
930  REM  GET PRINT LINE
940  L2$ = '' ''
950  L$ = '' ''
960  GET ZZ$
970  IF ZZ$ = CHR$ (13) THEN 1000
980  L$ = L$ + ZZ$
990  GOTO 960
1000 REM  CHOP UP LINE INTO CELLS
1010 IF  LEN (L$) >= LL * CW THEN 1040
1020 FOR K = LEN (L$) + 1 TO LL * CW
     :L$ = L$ + '' '': NEXT K
1030 L$ = LEFT$ (L$,LL * CW)
1040 FOR J = 1 TO LL
1050 ST$ = MID$ (L$,(J - 1) * CW + 1,CW)
1060 IF TR$(J) = ''L'' THEN 1090
1070 ST$ = LEFT$ (ST$,CW(J))
1080 GOTO 1100
1090 ST$ = RIGHT$ (ST$,CW(J))
1100 L2$ = L2$ + ST$
1110 NEXT J
1120 PR# 1: PRINT L2$;: PR# 0
1130 GOTO 930
1140 ERR = PEEK (222)
1150 IF ERR = 5 THEN 1170
1160 PRINT ''ERROR CODE '';ERR'':STOP
1170 PR# 1: PRINT CHR$ (13): PR# 0
1180 END
```

```
 10  REM  *********************
 20  REM  *                   *
 30  REM  *     VISIPRINT     *
 40  REM  *     BOB MOULD     *
 50  REM  *   OCTOBER 1983    *
 60  REM  * (MICROSOFT BASIC) *
 70  REM  * *******************
 80  REM
 90  REM  PROVIDES VARIABLE COL-
100  REM  COLUMN WIDTHS FOR
110  REM  VISICALC PRINTOUTS BY
120  REM  TRUNCATING CELL CONTENTS
130  REM
140  REM  .........................
150  DIM CD$(63),CW(63),TR$(63)
160  REM  READ VALID COLUMN DESIGNATORS
170  FOR J = 1 TO 26
180  READ CD$(J)
190  NEXT J
200  DATA  A,B,C,D,E,F,G,H,I,J,K,L,M,N,
          O,P,Q,R,S,T,U,V,W,X,Y,Z
210  FOR J = 27 TO 52
```

```
220  CD$(J! = ''A'' + CD$(J - 26)
230  NEXT J
240  FOR J = 53 TO 63
250  CD$(J) = ''B'' + CD$(J - 52)
260  NEXT J
270  REM
280  REM ......................
290  HOME
300  PRINT ''WHAT'S VISICALC PRINTOUT
       FILE NAME ''
310  INPUT F$
320  REM
330  REM  ASK FOR CURRENT NO.OF
340  REM  COLUMNS AND COLUMN WIDTH.
350  REM
360  PRINT ''HOW MANY COLUMNS '';
370  INPUT LL
380  IF LL > 0 THEN 420
390  PRINT : PRINT ''STOP MUCKING ABOUT!''
400  PRINT
410  GOTO 360
420  REM  GET CURRENT COLUMN WIDTH
430  PRINT
440  PRINT ''WHAT'S CURRENT COLUMN WIDTH '';
450  INPUT CW
460  REM  CALC CHARS IN LINE
470  CL = LL * CW
480  REM  SETUP ARRAY OF COLS AND WIDTHS
490  FOR J = 1 TO LL
500  CW(J) = CW
510  NEXT J
520  REM  GET NEW COLUMN WIDTHS
530  REM  ASSUME WIDTH=CURRENT WIDTH
540  REM  UNLESS OTHERWISE INPUT.
550  PRINT
560  PRINT ''GIVE THE FOLLOWING ONLY FOR
                      THOSE''
570  PRINT ''COLUMNS TO BE CHANGED :''
580  PRINT
590  PRINT ''COLUMN LETTER(S)''
600  PRINT ''NEW COLUMN WIDTH''
610  PRINT ''TRUNCATE ON LEFT (L) OR
                         RIGHT (R)''
620  PRINT
630  PRINT ''COLUMN (A TO BK)  :''
640  PRINT ''('END' TO EXIT)    :'';
650  INPUT NC$
660  IF NC$ = ''END'' THEN 890
670  PRINT ''NEW WIDTH        :'';
680  INPUT NW
690  PRINT ''TRUNCATE (L) OR (R) :'';
700  INPUT TR$
710  FOR J = 1 TO 63
720  IF NC$ = CD$(J) THEN 780
730  NEXT J
740  PRINT
750  PRINT  CHR$ (7)
760  PRINT ''INVALID COLUMN LETTER(S)''
770  GOTO 630
780  TR$(J) = TR$
790  FOR J = 1 TO LEN (NC$)
800  CN = 0
810  CN$ = MID$ (NC$,J,1)
820  IF CN$ = '' '' THEN 860
830  CN = CN + ASC (CN$) - 64
840  CN$ = '' ''
850  NEXT J
860  CW(CN) = NW
870  GOTO 620
880  REM  OPEN VISICALC PRINTOUT FILE
890  OPEN ''IN'',#1,F$
900  REM  GET PRINT LINE
910  L2$ = '' ''
920  IF EOF(1) THEN 1080
930  LINE INPUT#1,L$
940  REM  CHOP UP LINE INTO CELLS
950  IF LEN (L$) >= LL * CW THEN 980
960  FOR K = LEN (L$) + 1 TO LL * CW:
                 L$ = L$ + '' '': NEXT K
970  L$ = LEFT$ (L$,LL * CW)
980  FOR J = 1 TO LL
990  ST$ = MID$ (L$,(J - 1) * CW + 1,CW)
1000 IF TR$(J) = ''L'' THEN 1030
1010 ST$ = LEFT$ (ST$,CW(J))
1020 GOTO 1040
1030 ST$ = RIGHT$ (ST$,CW(J))
1040 L2$ = L2$ + ST$
1050 NEXT J
1060 LPRINT L2$;
1070 GOTO 900
1080 LPRINT  CHR$ (13)
1090 END
```

INDEX

TEMPLATES AVAILABLE ON DISK

The templates listed in this book are available for Apple II series computers on a 5¼-inch disk. The disk can save you hours of tedious key-boarding, giving more time to adapt, modify or experiment with the templates. To order your disk, complete the form below and send it directly to Cambridge University Press. RESIDENTS OF THE UNITED STATES AND CANADA PLEASE USE THE ORDER FORM ON THE OTHER SIDE.

To: Customer Services Department, Cambridge University Press, The Edinburgh Building, Shaftesbury Road, Cambridge, CB2 2RU

Please send me .... disk(s) 0 521 30744 9 containing templates from the book THE CAMBRIDGE GUIDE TO VISICALC by Bob Mould and Fran Teo at **£12.00** each (inclusive of VAT).

Name .... Block capitals please

Address ....

....

....

Please accept my payment by cheque or money order:

I enclose a Cheque (made payable to Cambridge University Press)/UK Postal Order/International Money Order/Bank Draft/Post Office Giro for £

Please accept my payment by credit card:

Charge my Barclaycard/VISA/Eurocard/Access/Mastercard/Bank Americard/ any other credit card bearing the Interbank symbol (please specify)

Card number | | | | | | | | | | | | | | | | Expiry date:

Signed:... Date:......................

Address as registered by card company:..

....

....

TEMPLATES AVAILABLE ON DISK

The templates listed in this book are available for Apple II series computers on a 5¼-inch disk. The disk can save you hours of tedious key-boarding, giving you more time to adapt, modify or experiment with the templates. To order your disk, please complete the form below and send it directly to Cambridge University Press.

RESIDENTS OF THE UNITED STATES AND CANADA PLEASE USE THIS FORM.

To: Mr Paul Wehn, Cambridge University Press,
32 East 57th Street, New York, N.Y. 10022

Please send me .... copies of the disk(s) 0 521 30744 9 containing templates from the book THE CAMBRIDGE GUIDE TO VISICALC by Bob Mould and Fran Teo at **$19.95** each.

Name .... Total price $............

Address .... Add NY/Calif tax ....

City .... Total $..........

State/Prov. .... Zip ....

.... VISA .... Mastercard .... Payment enclosed $............

Account No. .... MC 4-digit bank ....

Signature .... Expiration date ....

All individual orders must be prepaid or charged on VISA or Mastercard (libraries excepted). Cambridge University Press will pay postage. Residents of New York State and California, please add appropriate sales tax. Payment must be made in U.S. dollars or equivalent value in Canadian dollars.